Language and Situation
Language varieties and their social contexts

Language and Society

General editor

John Spencer
Director,
Institute of Modern English Language Studies,
University of Leeds

Language and Situation

Language varieties
and their social contexts

Michael Gregory and
Susanne Carroll

Routledge & Kegan Paul
London, Henley and Boston

First published in 1978 by
Routledge & Kegan Paul Ltd
39 Store Street, London WC1E 7DD
Broadway House, Newtown Road, Henley-on-Thames,
Oxon RG9 1EN and
9 Park Street, Boston, Mass. 02108, USA

Set in 10 on 11 point Times New Roman and
Printed in Great Britain by
Western Printing Services Ltd

British Library Cataloguing in Publication Data

Gregory, Michael

Language and situation. – (Language and
society).
1. Sociolinguistics
I. Title   II. Carroll, Susanne   III. Series
301.2′1   P40   77–30482

ISBN 0 7100 8756 X
ISBN 0 7100 8773 X Pbk

General editor's preface

When the linguist has described the structure of a language and codified its vocabulary, he has not taken us to the heart of the mystery. Of course, without grammars, lexicons and phonetic descriptions, we should understand nothing about the systems of languages. But these analyses inevitably stop short at the point where language, in serving personal and social ends, becomes part of the ceaseless flux of human life and activity. For we choose our utterances to fit situations, and text and context are therefore inter-related parts of a whole. Human communication cannot be comprehended without recognizing this mutual dependence. The mystery of language lies, if anywhere, in its endless ability to adapt both to the strategies of the individual and to the needs of the community, serving each without imprisoning either.

This is no new insight. Past scholars, especially those with close links with the study of society, like Boas and Sapir, Malinowski and J. R. Firth, have not failed to remind us of the necessary relation between the language we use and the situations within which we use it. In the past two decades, it is true, the focus of much linguistic inquiry has been upon languages viewed as homogeneous systems; and indeed, to probe more deeply into the nature of the 'rules' whereby well-formed sentences are produced, and the processes whereby human beings acquire these 'rules', is a worthy scientific endeavour. But equally, to explore the capacity of human beings to use language appropriately, and to select from their total linguistic repertoires those elements which match the needs of particular situations, is of complementary importance and interest—for meaning resides not in the forms of language but in their use.

However, when we try to observe language in use and attempt to systematize our observations and account for all the options, the task proves daunting. The matching halves of the equation

—language and context—are each variable in highly complex ways, and each requires delicate analysis. To unravel the web of inter-connections between them is a formidable endeavour. A sensitive 'way of looking', as well as an appropriately con-structed taxonomy of linked categories, is needed if a key is to be found to the intricate relationship between language systems and observable patterns of human behaviour and social inter-action.

Michael Gregory, now Professor of English at Glendon Col-lege in Toronto's York University, began to turn his attention to this problem fifteen years ago when he was at the University of Leeds. Since that time, as his subsequent publications indi-cate, he has continued to explore the nature of this complex connection between language variation and social contexts. Initially, the mainspring of his work was the British tradition that derived particularly from Malinowski and J. R. Firth, which stressed the relevance for meaning—indeed for our com-plete understanding of language—of the 'context of situation'. In a sense he still remains in that tradition, but he has un-doubtedly refined and widened it, making it both more rigorous and more catholic. Throughout his work he has been able to relate his own investigations of language in use, in Canada as well as in Britain and West Africa, to the theories and insights of other scholars from Europe, the USA and elsewhere.

With his collaborator and co-author, Susanne Carroll, he has now attempted a summation, an overall view, wide-ranging in scope yet delicately discriminating in detail. In the final chapter, the authors draw attention to the relevance of their framework of observation and reference for different aspects of linguistic study and research, and for the study of literature. Its practical value as well as its theoretical interest should make this work of considerable service to all who are engaged in the advanced study of language; and perhaps especially, though not exclu-sively, to those concerned with the study of English in all its manifold variety.

Socio-linguistics is a large and expanding field of inter-disciplinary activity, focusing attention in a variety of ways on the interaction of linguistic and social phenomena. For students in a broad range of human disciplines it can offer new and stimulating perspectives. It is the purpose of this series to offer brief, readable and scholarly introductions to the main themes and topics covered by current socio-linguistic studies.

John Spencer

Contents

Acknowledgments

The authors and publisher would like to thank the following for permission to reproduce copyright material: Cambridge University Press, for Tables 1, 2, and Figure 1, originally published in *Journal of Linguistics*, vol. 3; Walter de Gruyter, for extracts from M. A. K. Halliday, 'Text as Semantic Choice in Social Contexts', in T. A. Van Dijk and J. B. Petofi (eds), *Grammars and Descriptions* (1977); Glenlivet Distillers Ltd, Edinburgh; and McGraw-Hill for extracts from L. F. Edwards and C. R. L. Gaughram, *Concise Anatomy* (1971).

Chapter one

Introduction

> In the traffic of daily life, situations are constantly arising
> so closely similar that we do not hesitate to speak of them
> as the 'same situation'. Every language has its own fixed
> ways of coping with certain recurring situations.
> A. H. Gardiner, *The Theory of Speech and Language*

Among the various definitions distinguishing humanity from
other created beings is that of man as the 'talking animal'. The
inescapable fact—that 'man talks'—and the implications of
this human capacity, have been at the centre of investigation in
the linguistic sciences in the last couple of decades. Linguists
(such as Noam Chomsky) and psychologists (such as G. A.
Miller) have been concerned with the innate and, in many
respects, infinite capacity the human being has for language,
and much light has been thrown by such scholars both on the
nature of language and on the nature of being human. Such an
approach, emphasizing 'what the speaker knows' and concen-
trating on 'language as knowledge', has been characterized as
an intra-organism approach (Halliday, 1974).

Nevertheless, from another point of view it has to be remembered that in many crucial respects (such as 'what the speaker
does' and 'language as doing') what is more important is not so
much that 'man talks' as that 'men talk'; that is, that language
is essentially a social, an inter-organism, activity (Halliday,
op. cit.). We do not use it in isolation from the wider framework
of human activity, and even in the extreme case when we are
talking to ourselves, we still, in a sense, have company.

This book is written from the latter perspective on language,
which is a social one. It is concerned with what is involved in
looking at the language people really use (cf. Benson and
Greaves, 1973) talking or writing to each other at different
times, in different places, for different purposes, in different

social and personal contexts, and it is concerned with the mutual relations that can be seen to exist between different human social situations and different varieties of a language.

Of course, the notion that there is a strong and constant relationship between the language we use in a particular situation and certain features of that situation is no new one. It lies behind the rhetorics of ancient Greece and Rome, the medi-aeval lists of 'hard words', eighteenth-century English hand-books on Polite English, and the present series of technical dictionaries by Penguin Books: *Dictionary of Sailing*, *Dictionary of Psychology*, etc. However, to assert that we all use similar language in similar situations is not, of course, to claim that we all use the same language in the same situation. The claim is more modest but more important. It is not so naïve as to fail to recognize the ultimate uniqueness of any instance of language, but it is concerned with what any instance of language shares with some other instances, and the important predictability patterns that can be traced between situation and language. When we open a letter from our bank, a novel of Irving Wallace or indeed Graham Greene, go to hear a sermon or a political speech or read a *Times* editorial or *Time Magazine*, we have an idea of what we are going to get, and most times we more or less get what we expect. There is a match between language and social context, and it is the purpose of this book to be explicit about such matches and how we may talk about them.

So, with Catford (1965, p. 83), it will be assumed here that:

> the concept of a 'whole language' is so vast and heterogeneous that it is not operationally useful for many linguistic purposes, descriptive, comparative, and pedagogical. It is therefore desirable to have a framework of categories for the classification of 'sub-languages' or varieties within a total language.

This book is based on such a framework as it has been developed in the past fifteen years or so, particularly by British scholars (cf. Halliday, McIntosh and Strevens, 1964; Enkvist,

Spencer and Gregory, 1964; Catford, 1965; Gregory, 1967, 1969; Halliday, 1974, 1975a, 1975b, forthcoming); but it has similarities with work on the ethnology of communication by Dell Hymes and others in the USA (cf. Hymes, 1967). Though regarded as being relevant to languages in general, the framework of insights and categories presented here will be largely applied to, and exemplified from, English.

The first assumption we make is that the idea we have of 'language' or 'a language' is related to our knowledge and observation of, and participation in, actual occurrences of language—what are called language events. Most of these events, occurring as they do within the complex and continuing process of social activity are, of course, sequential and transitory, and are thus not readily amenable to investigation at the time of their actual occurrence. So we have to have recourse to records of these events through our memory, through informed recognition of what is likely in the particular language, and through the use of sound-recordings or of scripts, written either in conventional orthography or in some form of phonetic notation. Any such record, recalled, sound-recorded, written or printed, of a language event, is known as a text: it is both a physical thing and a semantic unit; and it is what happens in language in action.

Language is transmitted; it is patterned, and it is embedded in the human social experience. So it is both possible and useful to discern three crucial aspects of a language event—the substantial, the formal, and the situational. The transmission of language is by means of audible sound waves or visible marks on a surface. This is the substance of the language event, which is either phonic (audible sounds) or graphic (visible signs).

In bits of phonic or graphic substance that are instances of language, and not mere babbling or scribbling, there are discernible patterns, regularities in internal relations which go beyond mere similarities in sound or vision; in other words, the patterns are more than just patterns of substance. They are, rather, patterns *in* substance which are meaningful in terms of our human social behaviour and our understanding of it—as in the comparable yet contrastive grammatical and vocabulary patterns of

He's gone to the game.
Has she gone to the store?

This internal meaningful structure is known as form.

Now it is also observable that language events do not occur in isolation from other aspects of human behaviour; rather, we know that they operate within the manifold complex of human social behaviour and are mutually related to it. They take place in situations, and situation is the third aspect of the language event: 'the environment in which text comes to life' (Halliday, 1975b). For the moment, situation can be thought of as the relevant extra-textual circumstances, linguistic and non-linguistic, of the language event/text in question.

These, therefore, are the three essential aspects of the language event: substance, which is either phonic (audible sound waves) or graphic (visible, or in the case of Braille, tactile, marks on a surface); form, its meaningful internal patterning; and situation, its relevant extra-textual circumstances, linguistic and non-linguistic. These aspects of the language event are relatable to the levels or strata of language and linguistic description (cf. Halliday, forthcoming; Lamb, 1966). The lexico-grammatical level (syntax, morphology and vocabulary) is concerned with form; semantic statements correlate the contextual relations between situation and form; and phonology links form and substance, attempting to be explicit about how sounds and features of sound are utilized in a given language in order to realize the meaningful contrasts of grammar and lexis.

A framework for understanding and describing language varieties has to deal with the *constant* features of the situational circumstances of language events that can be consistently related to variety in the language texts. Such features fall into two main groups: one group relates to reasonably permanent characteristics of the user in language events, the other relates to the user's use of language in such events; and they yield the two main kinds of language variety that will be discussed in this book: dialects and diatypes.

'A language variety is a sub-set of formal and/or substantial features which correlates regularly with a particular type of socio-situational feature' (Catford, 1965, p. 84). A variety category is then a contextual category correlating groupings of linguistic features with recurrent situational features. So there is needed a set of situational categories for the description of those socio-situational features which correlate with sub-sets of linguistic features.

Now when we talk about Mr X's English or Miss Y's English we are referring to the language varieties of different users of English and recognizing that our individuality is, as it must be, reflected in our language—that 'the style is', to an extent, 'the man'. Most of us can detect our friends in what they speak and write, and this is not just because of the sound of their voice or the look of their handwriting. It is also because they have favourite grammatical structures, pronunciations, pitch and stress patterns, and vocabulary items. The situational category we need to handle this aspect of language behaviour is user's individuality, and the set of linguistic features associated with a particular person constitutes his/her 'individual dialect' or idiolect.

Terms like Old English, Middle English, Elizabethan English and Modern English recognize that language varies along the dimension of time and the appropriate situational category in this instance is user's temporal provenance (place in time), and the related set of linguistic features constitutes a temporal dialect.

Contrasts and comparisons between British and American English, on the other hand, indicate that the place in which we learnt and customarily use English is reflected in what we speak and write. Geographical provenance and geographical dialect are the related categories.

In the 1950s an attempt was made to distinguish between U and non-U English, that is Upper Class and non-Upper Class English (Ross, 1954, 1956), and in the eighteenth and nineteenth centuries it was customary for scholars to distinguish Polite from Vulgar English. Such distinctions, when valid, reflect the relationship between language and social class.

Social provenance of users and social dialect are appropriate categories for looking at such relationships.

There remains another type of dialect distinction which it is useful to make for a language that is spoken in many different and differing communities, not always with inter-intelligibility. This is the distinction between a standard and a non-standard dialect. Standard dialect need not have a simple or direct reference to the influence of particular social or geographical provenances, nor is it just a matter of accent. The term is needed to indicate, where that is appropriate, what has been called 'the universal form' of a language (Abercrombie, 1955, p. 11): that set of semantic, grammatical, lexical and phonological patterns which enables certain users of English (for example) throughout the English-speaking world to communicate intelligibly with each other. So user's range of intelligibility is the related situational category: and like all other dimensions of situation variation which correlate with language variety this, too, is a continuum (or cline) of variation rather than a series of discrete steps, although it is useful to make distinctions such as standard, sub-standard, non-standard, to mark points along the cline.

Today, standard English has world-wide currency, being spoken in varying accents, and written by, Englishmen, Welshmen, Irishmen and Scots; by Americans, Canadians, Australians, New Zealanders, West Indians, Rhodesians and South Africans; and by many other people, in Black Africa and the Indian sub-continent, for whom it may not be a mother tongue. Of course there are grammatical and vocabulary differences amongst the standard Englishes throughout the world but they need not be significant in relation to the standard/non-standard contrast.

All the varieties discussed so far, which are known as dialectal varieties or dialects (summarized in Table 1), have a long history of recognition and use in philological and linguistic scholarship. They are, as has been noted, concerned with the linguistic reflections of reasonably permanent characteristics of the user, a necessary and constant feature of situations in which there are language events. The qualification of 'permanent' with 'reasonably' is not unimportant because, although a user's individuality, temporal, geographical and social provenances, and range of intelligibility within the wider speech community all have a high degree of constancy, it is of course possible for a language user to assume, at least partially and temporarily, the linguistic habits of another individual, or time, or place, or social class for reasons of parody, art, humour, etc., or indeed to assume them unconsciously as a result of linguistic social accommodation. For example, many English speakers and many Canadian speakers of French, in particular, control both a standard and a non-standard dialect: the selection of one rather than another in different situations being related to questions of use—particularly relationships with the hearer or reader, the type of situation variation yielding diatypic varieties or diatypes—the linguistic reflection of the user's use of language in situations (Table 2).

The three major dimensions of such variation are contextually categorized as field, mode and tenor of discourse. In a general sense they are all related to the role being played by the user in the language event. Field of discourse is the consequence of the user's purposive role, what his language is 'about', what experience he is verbalizing, what is 'going on' through language. This includes, of course, topic and subject matter and reflects Gardiner's point (1932, p. 98) that in speech events participants are revealing 'an intelligible purpose'. Some non-specialist purposive roles such as 'establishing personal contact' or 'phatic communion' (cf. Malinowski, 1923; Firth, 1957) have a number of possible related topics such as 'weather', 'health', 'projected holidays', 'current news'. The specialized roles of scientist, technologist, expert, and informed enthusiast, relate to specialist fields, and are more likely to have a one-to-one field relationship.

An important initial distinction in classifying a language such as English according to field of discourse might be between what are called Technical Englishes and non-Technical Englishes, between, that is, those Englishes in which the field-purposive role correlation so determines the language used that it becomes rather restricted to that role and to those acquainted with it (e.g. the English of Mathematics, Legal English, the English of Linguistics), and those Englishes which are not so restricted.

The mode of discourse is the linguistic reflection of the relationship the language user has to the medium of transmission. Initially, this relationship may be seen as the simple one of which medium is being used: speech or writing. However, as soon as relationships such as those between conversation in real life and dialogue in novels and plays, or between a speech and an article, are considered, then more delicate distinctions are necessary, and differences between spontaneous and non-spontaneous speech, and between what is written to be spoken and what is written 'to be read with the eye', become relevant.

The relationship the user has with his audience, his adressee(s), is the situational factor that is involved in tenor of discourse. Tenors of discourse result from the mutual relations between the language used and the relationships among the participants in language events. When the relationship is considered on the personal axis, variations ranging from extreme degrees of formality through norms to extreme degrees of informality are what are relevant, and the user's personal addressee relationship and personal tenor of discourse are appropriate general categories. However, there are also variations related to what the user is trying to *do* with language (in a sense that is different from the purposive-role/field-of-discourse factors) for, or to, his addressee(s)—whether he is teaching, persuading, advertising, amusing, controlling, etc. Functional addressee relationship and functional tenor of discourse are the categories to cope with this constant source of significant situational and linguistic variation.

Categories such as user's individuality, temporal provenance, geographical provenance, social provenance, range of intelligibility, purposive role, medium relationships and personal and functional addressee relationship are, then, general situational categories for the description of language events. They pattern with idiolect, temporal, geographical, social, standard and non-standard dialects, field, mode, and personal and functional tenors of discourse, which are general contextual categories when they are applied to a particular language. Old and Middle English, Legal English and Medical English, Spoken and and Middle Class English, Standard and non-Standard English, Legal English and Medical English, Spoken and Written English, Formal and Informal English, Advertising English and Didactic English, are descriptive categories, instances of dialects and diatypes in a particular language.

The linguistic component of a realized, descriptive contextual category attempts to delineate its indexical markers (the grammatical, lexical, phonological/graphological features peculiar to, and characteristic of, itself) and to give some indication of its common-core features (those it shares with one or more other varieties). Such exemplified descriptive contextual categories are, then, statements of what Firth (1964, p. 173) called 'common verbalizations' of 'common situational contexts' and 'experiential contexts' of the users of the language. Their description is central to any practical or applied semantics. Part of the competence of the users of a particular language can be seen to be their awareness of these common verbalizations of common experiences and situations and this enables the texts of language events to create their own situations themselves, to call into relevancy extra-textual features not within the perceptually present situation, which is why language can operate endophorically (i.e. independently of the immediate situation) as well as exophorically (i.e. related to non-linguistic circumstances).

There remains one other important category of language variation. Many texts can be located roughly on the same points on the clines of field, mode and tenors. For example: 'lectures (modes and tenors) on geography (field)', 'sermons (field, mode and tenors)', 'cooking (field) recipe (tenors) books (mode)', 'personal (field and tenors) conversations (tenor and mode)'. These represent registers: the varieties according to use of which a text may be regarded as an instance. As has been aptly pointed out (Halliday, 1974):

Table 1 Suggested categories of dialectal variety differentiation

	Situational categories	Contextual categories	Examples of English varieties (descriptive contextual categories)	
user's	individuality	idiolect	Mr X's English, Miss Y's English	Dialectal varieties: the linguistic reflection of reasonably permanent characteristics of the *user* in language situations
	temporal provenance	temporal dialect	Old English, Modern English	
	geographical provenance	geographical dialect	British English, American English	
	social provenance	social dialect	Upper Class English, Middle Class English	
	range of intelligibility	standard/ non-standard dialect	Standard English, non-Standard English	

Source: Gregory (1967).

Table 2 Suggested categories of diatypic variety differentiation

	Situational categories	Contextual categories	Examples of English varieties (descriptive contextual categories)	
user's	purposive role	field of discourse	Technical English, non-Technical English	Diatypic varieties: the linguistic reflection of recurrent characteristics of user's *use* of language in situations
	medium relationship	mode of discourse	Spoken English, Written English	
	addressee relationship	tenor of discourse		
	(a) personal	personal tenor	Formal English, Informal English	
	(b) functional	functional tenor	Didactic English, non-Didactic English	

Source: Gregory (1967).

there is not a great deal one can predict about the language that will be used if one knows *only* the field of discussion or *only* the mode or the tenor. But if we know all these we can predict quite a lot.

Equally interesting are the semantic implications of the concept of register. A register can be seen as (Halliday, 1975b, p. 26):

> a configuration of the semantic resources that the member of a culture typically associates with a situation type. It is the meaning potential that is deployed in a given social context. It thus represents the semantic options, and combinations of semantic options, that are 'at risk' under particular environmental conditions.

This, and other aspects of the place of language varieties in a theory of the semantics of language use, will be discussed in Chapters six and eight.

Chapter two

Dialect

Cornwall: What mean'st by this?
Kent: To go out of my dialect, which you discommend
so much.
King Lear

Those characteristic features of language which we relate to different users of a language are categorized as dialectal. By this term we make no reference to the 'quality' of a variety; a dialect is not necessarily less complete, less logical, less 'language' than a language. Ranking varieties in terms of aesthetic or psychological traits has not proved to be productive or enlightening, for the notion of linguistic 'goodness' has been shown to be nebulous. There seems to be no objective, culturally non-biased way of measuring it (Martinet, 1965). So it is not the custom in linguistics to use the term dialect as a pejorative term for 'lesser' types of language (cf. Haugen, 1966); we will be using it to refer to the relationships of language habits with the speaker's place on dimensions of individuality, time, place, social class and speech community.

If the non-specialist public have a tendency to think of dialect as language's poor country cousin, they also tend to confuse dialect and accent. Accent normally refers to articulatory and acoustic features of language while dialect refers to the totality of lexical, grammatical and phonological features. Dialect therefore incorporates accent but remains distinct from it. It can be thought of as the user's macro-linguistic identity defining him in terms of birthplace, class, education and age. So while a person's accent may initially be the most striking aspect of his language, that of which we are consciously and immediately aware, it comprises only a part of the variation possible.

Temporal dialects

The categorization of language into temporal dialects is a traditional, and seemingly natural, part of linguistic study. When we read *Sir Gawain and the Green Knight*, or a play by G. B. Shaw, we are aware of varying differences between our own language and that of both the authors; differences which cannot be attributed entirely to *genre* or to the peculiarities of the authors' styles. The indexical markers may be subtle differences in meaning or they may be quite glaring grammatical distinctions. The following passage from Shakespeare's *Romeo and Juliet* may illustrate (Act I, sc. 1):

> *Sampson:* Gregory, o' my word, we'll not carry coals.
> *Gregory:* No, for then we should be colliers.
> *Sampson:* I mean, an we be in choler we'll draw.
> *Gregory:* Ay, while you live, draw your neck out o' the collar.
> *Sampson:* I strike quickly, being mov'd.
> *Gregory:* But thou art not quickly mov'd to strike.
> *Sampson:* A dog of the house of Montague moves me.
> *Gregory:* To move is to stir, and to be valiant is to stand, therefore if thou art mov'd, thou runn'st away.

The distinction of second-person polite and second-person informal as realized in the pronominal contrast 'thou'/'you' and its corresponding verb forms 'art'/'runn'st' and 'are'/'run' no longer exists in modern English. Where these forms are used distinctively today they are related to a stylistic decision for or against archaism. Less obvious perhaps is the use of the word 'house' for 'family' and the prepositional phrase 'of Montague' for the pre-placed possessive form 'Montague's house'. The punning centring on the various meanings of 'move' also seems a little dated. The meaning of the passage is, however, reasonably transparent in spite of features such as 'an' (modern English 'if'). The same could not be said for the following text from Old English (Early English Text Society, 1891, pp. 220–1):

Þissum tidum Middlengle Peadan Pendan sunu þæs
cyniges Cristes geleafan ⁊ sodfæstnisse geryne enfengen.
Waes he Peada ging ædeling good ⁊ cyninges nomon ⁊
hada welwyrde; ⁊ se fæder him fordon rice fesealde
þære þeode.

The Germanic origins of English are perhaps more evident in
this second text, a fact which unfortunately does not render
the text more comprehensible for most contemporary users of
English. It needs translating:

At this time the Middle Angles, with Peada, son of
King Penda, received the faith of Christ and the mysteries
of the truth. Paeda was an excellent young prince, well
worthy of the name and rank of king; and for this reason
his father made over to him the government of that
people.

Both these texts are written, and much of our understanding
of temporal dialects comes from an examination of the written
word. This technique has its limitations since we can gain only
limited information about the sound systems of earlier periods
(from such features as variation in spellings, and spelling
'errors') and since we do not have available for study those
language activities which were not deemed worthy of written
record. Naturally the study of pre-literate language remains
speculative. Linguistics has therefore greatly benefited from the
development of tape-recording techniques which capture what
is said as it is spoken. Such techniques have made for more
accurate articulatory and prosodic phonetics and have permitted a more rapid development of the study of language
variation, intra- and inter-individual.

Language forms a continuum in time so that when we look
back at a given period it is not possible to determine precisely
when one temporal dialect begins and another ends. Diachronic variation, the variable use of features from two different
temporal dialects, must occur as change spreads. Traditionally,
linguists have maintained that such change could not be
directly observed. At best, it was felt, only the successive stages

of the progression could be observed, much in the way we note that the hands of a clock have moved without seeing the movement. However, recent work on pidgins and creoles (and what has been called by some 'the post-creole continuum') has led to the development of dynamic models of language. Instead of relegating variables to a 'free variation' waste-basket, specific features are now being described in terms of the trends they typify, particularly as features spread from age group to age group, or class to class (cf. Bickerton, 1973; Smith, 1973). By looking at the differences in dialects of different periods and at the differences in the speech of successive generations the linguist can determine whether a variable is spreading or receding in the community.

Descriptive terms like 'Old', 'Modern' or 'Contemporary' English do not, then, refer to exact periods of time but rather to progressive stages of development. These epithets are used as well to categorize temporal varieties of other languages at quite different dates. Old English is reputed to have ended at about 1150 but Old French was still spoken in the 1300s. Because the impetus for linguistic change is embedded in the social matrix, change will be dependent on the kinds of social pressures exerted upon various sub-groups. The evolutionary timetables for different languages will therefore be culturally determined and not coterminous.

Change may be sudden and abrupt, like the generalization of aeronautic jargon in American English: 'take-off', 'blast-off', 'spacewalk', and so on. It may also be gradual—the angliciz-ation of some minority groups in the northern parts of Canada or its West has taken several generations because of their relative isolation and the institutional independence of their anglophone neighbours. Change may originate in the upper echelons or in the lower: 'franglais' in France, the borrowing of English lexical items and pronunciations, is largely a middle-class phenomenon, but in Canada it begins largely in the lower class.

Change affects us all as individuals and as members of social groups. Our language develops as we do; we do not speak at fifty as we did at five. The ageing politician trying to impress his younger constituents with his capacity to understand their problems may pepper his discourse with expressions and slang from a succeeding generation. His attempts at 'image-building' testify to associations of language and philosophy, language and behaviour. Differences in language will reflect increased knowledge (learning about baseball or *haute cuisine* involves learning how to talk about them), or greater experience, personal ambitions, and individual mobility (so that if we want to fit into a group we will model our language, consciously or unconsciously, along appropriate lines).

If language change is viewed as a type of evolutionary process it cannot be interpreted as being determined entirely by 'natural', universal laws. On the contrary, we have suggested that change is rooted in social processes. This is illustrated by the development of pidgins and creoles. Pidgins are structurally simplified, functionally undifferentiated languages which develop in contact situations between linguistically disparate groups. This contact situation is different from other kinds (immigration, conquest, etc.) in that individual bilingual intermediaries are lacking, so that inter-group communication depends upon the use of a simplified 'mixed' language. In certain situations the pidgin can become the mother tongue of some element of the groups involved. This necessitates lexical expansion and functional differentiation of the pidgin. The new language resulting from this process is the creole (cf. Todd, 1974). Pidgins and creoles have often been looked upon as only marginally interesting but are now evoking great interest among linguists because they indicate some of the processes by which change occurs at the individual level and at the level of the community. They provide excellent examples of diachronic, or temporal, and synchronic variation (regional or social variation within a given temporal framework) (cf. Smith, 1973).

Geographical dialect

One of the most readily recognizable of linguistic traits is regional 'accent'—we notice immediately this feature of dialect. For many the term dialect refers first and foremost to regional or geographical variation, whether one is referring to British, American, Indian or Nigerian English; and often it is opposed to 'language'. However, a close examination of the structural differences between 'languages' like Dutch, German and Danish and 'dialects' like Swiss or Austrian German reveals that the distinction sometimes may be more political, historical or cultural than linguistic.

In examining geographical variation we might tend to assume that each of the varieties in question has the same status or function in the region where it is spoken. So we assume that there is a British, American or Canadian English spoken by a relatively homogeneous, monolingual population. This is, of course, a fiction. There are regional dialects of British, American and Canadian English within these broad categorizations. In some communities where English is spoken as an 'other' language the fiction is more obvious. In India and in West Africa there are sub-groups whose mother tongue is English, but by and large the vast majority of English-speakers has acquired English as a second (possibly third or fourth) language. But in these societies English is not a 'foreign' language with models being borrowed from other nations (as is, for example, French in Great Britain). Rather, English is one of several languages spoken, and a local regional variety serves as the local standard. In some areas, alongside this local standard there exist, as well, local non-standard varieties, which may be creoles or pidgins. Sometimes the regional standard represents a social dialect spoken by the élite. It may also be appropriate for certain fields—for example, administration, science or war —in which case the dialectal variety assumes diatypic functions.

These uses reflect a social continuum (cf. Social dialect) but the distinctions between geographical varieties normally reflect physical space between speakers and between communities. It is this space which prevents social interaction and permits the development of distinct linguistic features. The variation may be slight as one passes from one village to the next because physical space relationships can themselves frequently be seen as comprising a continuum. It can also be quite dramatic if one passes into a dialect enclave or crosses over a dialect boundary. These borders or isoglosses are perhaps more evident and more 'real' than the physical or administrative boundaries which we assign to geographical areas. But to the extent that the physical border inhibits social interaction it may be paralleled by a linguistic border.

When we consider the question of dialects and languages in terms of the attitudes that we acquire (the Texas 'twang' or the Tennessee 'drawl', 'pure' Parisian French or New Brunswick 'chiak') the distinctions between languages and dialects become more than problematic. To the newly independent state attempting to foster viable national symbols the choice of which regional dialect or which tribal language to elevate to the status of official language can be crucial. Favouring the language of one group over that of another can often produce internal division; and this may be true even if structurally the varieties in question are similar but with differences which reflect existing social divisions. The numerous language riots in India, in opposition to making Hindi the official language, offer ample evidence of local resistance to government language policy. The impassioned resistance of Basque groups, on the other hand, reveals how important official recognition, and its guarantees against enforced assimilation, can be.

Social dialect

As time and physical dimensions are reflected in language, so too is social 'space'. The organization of people into different groups is realized in the differentiation of language into social dialects such as U (upper-class) and non-U in British English, or lower- and middle-class American or Canadian English. The acquisition of a given social dialect depends on one's membership in a class which may be determined by birth, education, profession, wealth, race or religion. Social status, depending upon the society in question, can be achieved or ascribed, revealing horizontal or vertical divisions. Therefore in India one's personal status was traditionally largely circum-scribed at birth by caste membership. In Britain birth, education and profession were defining factors allowing for some individual mobility; and in America, although one once distinguished between 'old money' (good) and the *'nouveau riche'* (less good), wealth was equally important in defining status. Linguistically what one says will largely be determined by where one fits in the hierarchy. Ross's original studies on U and non-U (1954, 1956) were designed to reveal in fact how, in spite of possessing many of the other accoutrements of upper-class membership, middle-class speakers would inevitably 'slip', showing their origins.

While absolute markers distinguishing social dialects may exist, recent work suggests that the differences between social dialects may not rest in self-monitoring and in varying perceptions of situation-appropriate language. Labov (1972b) has studied a number of socially significant variables in American English, like *th* and *ing*, and has found that usage does indeed vary across classes. Highest frequencies of usage for the prestige form $/\theta/$ rather than $/t^h/$ and $/i\eta/$ rather than $/+n/$ were recorded by speakers in the higher end of the socioeconomic scale, and lowest frequencies were recorded by speakers in the lower ends. This confirms the validity of the markers. However, a great deal of intra-individual variation occurred which cut across class divisions. All groups increased their use of prestige variables in formal discourse and reading styles and revealed the least amount of self-monitoring in informal discourse. This suggests that perception for the need for style-shifts can spread across class lines and that all classes will tend to associate the same social markers with the situational variables.

Mass media and universal education have contributed to developing a tolerance of regional variations and at the same time 'ironing out' major differences. There is evidence, however, that the same process is not occurring with respect to social dialects. This may reflect in part the fact that U-speakers or middle-class speakers will use non-prestige features in informal discourse (the social dialects therefore share many more features than different regional dialects). It may also be that while the bonds linking an individual to a specific region have been weakened (by industrialization and urbanization and by the increased physical mobility of modern man) those bonds linking him to social groups have not. Recent psychological testing (Lambert, 1967; Labov, 1972b) reveals that linguistic attitudes with respect to socially significant variables are generalized throughout the community. Speakers who use stigmatized variables seem unaware of this fact and possess the same negative attitudes towards their own language as do other speakers. It seems, however, that attitudes are not uniformly negative and undifferentiated. While users may devalue their own dialect with respect to 'performance' values (personal success, upward mobility, competence, etc.) they may attribute positive 'ethical' values to these same markers (values like honesty, toughness, strength, sincerity, etc.). This differentiation may then contribute to reinforcing group identification and loyalty.

Nevertheless overt changes can and do occur which reveal a growing tolerance of stereotypic features of social dialect. Prior to 1960, for example, BBC policy limited the use of regional working-class accents to character parts. Since then there has been a move away from a *de rigueur* use of RP. (Received Pronunciation or RP is the term traditionally used by phoneticians to refer to the socially prestigious British accent associated with upper-class and upper middle-class speech.) Similarly in the same post-1960 period Britain's stage English has also come to incorporate non-U accents. Albert Finney, Nicol Williamson, Judi Dench and Tom Courtenay have played major stage roles (including classic ones such as Hamlet, Juliet and Henry V) with accents, regionally and to some extent socially marked, that Sir John Gielgud, Dame Peggy Ashcroft and Sir Ralph Richardson would not have dreamt of using twenty years before.

Because a number of factors can determine the nature of social stratification the crucial variable in distinguishing a person's social dialect may be profession, or religion or race. The ghettoization of American blacks in cities in the northern US led to the development of distinctive patterns of social interaction and, incidentally, to the development of a distinctive variety of English commonly referred to as non-standard Black English (NBE). It was the economic, cultural and political isolation of the blacks from the centre of American life which helped create this particular variety. And yet although NBE is associated with race it is a function of ghetto life. Middle-class blacks do not speak NBE nor do southern blacks (so NBE is neither just a product of race nor of education). The dialect has traditionally been viewed as a hindrance to full integration into white society, so much effort has been spent trying to teach ghetto children standard American English. Ironically enough, the dialect has acquired greater prestige in becoming an authentic symbol of black culture; and perhaps even more ironically, the greater militancy of blacks and their recent successes have increased their prestige so that for bottom members of the social scale Black English can be a suitable model (particularly if this group does not consist of native-speakers of English). Wolfram (1973) has found that Puerto Ricans living in the ghettos incorporate non-standard features into their speech which cannot be attributed to Spanish interference. Rather, some of the distinctive markers of Puerto Rican English can be traced to borrowing from NBE.

Standard dialect

Social and standard dialects are often confused because they are interpreted only in terms of prestige. While there is a tendency to assume that the 'best' speech is spoken by the upper classes and that the standard dialect must be the 'best' speech, studies done on variable use of prestige features in American English show that the lower middle class has a tendency to use more prestige forms in formal discourse than does the upper middle class (Labov, 1972b). Labov has referred to this tendency as 'hypercorrection' and sees in it an important element in the propagation of linguistic change (*op. cit.*, pp. 122–42).

Because we have defined standard dialect in terms of intelligibility, we can suggest that it would be entirely possible for all members of a community to speak a standard variety regardless of their social standing. It is therefore understandable that when the British survey of English dialects was undertaken after the Second World War some difficulty was had in finding non-standard speakers (Orton, 1962). The non-standard rural dialects had largely disappeared since the First World War.

Standardization is not simply a question of numbers, of being that variety spoken by the most populous segment of the community. Standardization is normally linked to some kind of institutional support, perhaps in the form of universal education, media, the growth and spread of government administration or of armies. Inherent in the process is the normalization and codification of the language. Normalization and codification may be performed by universities, academies, scientific and technical bodies, regulatory committees and so on. When, for example, a trade union stipulates that in all contracts and official documents specific functions will be designated in a given manner and that people performing those functions will be called by certain names, it is performing a standardizing function. This is particularly important where the trade union has national rather than just local influence. This same function is performed by individuals who write grammars and books on correct usage and who help to develop positive attitudes towards the norm (cf. Garvin, 1959).

What a speaker says on any occasion is in part, as we have stressed, a reflection of his social identity. This is true in a double sense—through the dialects the speaker uses and also through the code(s) he possesses. Code (see Chapter seven) refers to what verbal behaviour the speaker considers as situation-appropriate, the behavioural options which the speaker can put into play. These options have been called 'strategies of use' and determine when we deem it appropriate to speak or to remain silent, to interpret meaning as context-bound or context-free. Some North American Indians, for instance, do not use the same verbal strategies as do whites and the consequences of this can be serious for their children, particularly those attending white schools (cf. Basso, 1970; Philips, 1972). Bernstein (1971, 1973) has suggested that British middle-class and working-class children possess different types of code and this affects the academic success of the working-class children. Focusing on language as the medium of socialization, Bernstein suggests that different kinds of meaning are made available to working-class and middle-class children and he therefore attempts to establish a relationship between the formal features of social dialect and code. At another level of interpretation, then, it is the social order which is determining the ways in which meaning is encoded in language, determining which kinds of meaning are made available to which groups and also determining which kinds of verbal behaviour will be rewarded.

Idiolect

Idiolect differs from other categories in that it reflects all of them at once. The uniqueness of an individual's speech comes not by abstracting features of temporal, geographical, social and standard or non-standard dialect but rather from the configuration of these features.

Idiolect is a more 'accessible' variety than the others since abstractions made are characteristic of a single speaker and not those features shared by many. This 'accessibility', however, does not make idiolect easier to isolate and describe. On the contrary, linguistic individuality may be more difficult to isolate simply because it is the consequence of the inter-relationships of the other dialects and of the range of diatypes controlled by the individual.

Most of us will recognize favourite expressions that we use habitually or that we hear others using. But we may also have preferences or tendencies to use specific syntactic forms and typical pronunciations. Looking at an isolated segment from the Appendix, we note that while both speakers are asking questions and requesting information, D seems to prefer interrogatives using modals and rising intonation, Wh- constructions, or inversion and rising intonation:

D: do you want any more↗
D: do you want me to hand you the thing Gilles↗
D: what can I do for you↗
D: can I help you↗

S, on the other hand, seems to prefer structurally simplified utterances where interrogation is marked only by intonation:

S: two↗
S: coffee↗
S: oui, Marie↗

These examples are cited merely to illustrate how speech can vary between individuals. The isolation and description of an idiolect would naturally require a detailed examination of a much larger corpus.

Variation in individual speech can also be part and parcel of learning another language. Since most of us know our mother tongue better than a second language, we are likely to borrow structures, words and meanings from our first language as we learn the second (L_2). At the same time bilinguals may be less likely to naturalize elements borrowed from other languages and may introduce foreign lexical items into their discourse.

When a person attempts to become bilingual he must learn new rules which constitute the L_2 (rules encoding and organizing meaning into sound). When interference occurs it indicates that the learning process is incomplete. The learner may also produce utterances which are aberrant but which cannot be said to be interference. These may be produced because the learner has developed intermediate rules, what Selinker (1974) has called 'interlanguage' and Nemser (1974) has termed 'approximate systems'. As a speaker becomes more fluent in the L_2 his rule-governed output, his interlanguage, will replicate to an increasing degree what the native speaker would use.

Variation within an idiolect will also reflect developmental processes of the individual as he 'learns' his own language. It will reflect personal experience certainly and also changes in values and ideology. The things we do and the activities we indulge in will influence the choice of words we use. The *vendeuse* whose sales pitch includes epithets like 'fabulous', 'stunning' or 'superb', expects those words to produce a specific effect on a client. But the choice between those words and saying, 'Oh, isn't that nice!' will undoubtedly reflect the personality of the individual implicated.

As change occurs at the social level it will be reflected in the way the individual chooses to express himself. The 'four-letter word' is no longer restricted to back rooms or to the boys who inhabit them. Nice ladies are no longer defined by their avoidance of 'foul' language. In a similar vein minority groups and 'libbers', aware of the psychological power of denigratory terms like 'nigger', 'wop' or 'Mick' approach the problem of changing attitudes at the level of individual speech. Hence the activity of anti-defamation leagues and those who would rid us of the word 'man'.

It would be difficult to describe an idiolect on the basis of a single text or even from texts taken from a single period of a person's life. In a sense we possess several styles over the course of a lifetime, each one a typical reflection of our individuality.

Normally an unconscious reflection of experience, idiolect can also be manipulated, like other variables, for creative, humorous purposes. The mimic selects and often exaggerates those features we associate with a famous celebrity, and for the writer, the conscious perfection of literary style is a necessary part of the craft. The conscious style can take on an existence in addition to idiolect when the latter becomes parody or caricature. Lillian Ross (1961, pp. 57–8), in her biography of Ernest Hemingway, may have done more to perpetuate the myth than to expose the reality, notably the public image of Hemingway as the tough novelist emanating *machismo*:

> I began to learn to read French by reading the A.P.
> story in the French paper after reading the American A.P.
> story, and finally learned to read it by reading accounts
> of things I had seen—les événements sportifs—and from
> that and les crimes it was only a jump to Dr. de
> Maupassant, who wrote about things I had seen or could
> understand. Dumas, Daudet, Stendhal, who when I
> read him I knew that was the way I wanted to be able
> to write. Mr. Flaubert who always threw them perfectly
> straight, hard, high and inside. Then Mr. Baudelaire, that
> I learned my knuckle ball from, and Mr. Rimbaud, who
> never threw a fast ball in his life. Mr. Gide and

Mr. Valéry I couldn't learn from. I think Mr. Valéry was too smart for me. Like Jack Britton and Benny Leonard.

Variation is a natural part of everyday linguistic intercourse. We change our habits to accommodate the people who surround us and to meet the circumstances in which we find ourselves. This is the type of variation which will concern us in the rest of this book—diatypic variation; language-in-situation. But let us not forget that what we say is an indication of who we are as individuals, although even as unique persons our habits are neither fixed nor stable but mirror the constant variability of environment and attitude which makes up our lives.

Chapter three

Fields of discourse

> Descriptive linguistics is at its best when it concentrates
> on what I call restricted languages. A restricted language
> serves a circumscribed field of experience or action and
> can be said to have its own grammar and dictionary.
> J. R. Firth, *Selected Papers*

Because of the centrality of language in our human and social experience, scholars from diverse disciplines concerned with behaviour have attempted to form theories of language; and because linguistic behaviour is a highly meaningful kind of 'doing', many of these theories have been functional in nature, that is they have generalized about language *in use*. From anthropology and ethnology there has been the work of Malinowski (1923, 1935) and Morris (1967); from psychology that of Bühler (1934), and from social educational theory that of Britton (1970) and Bernstein (1971, 1973, 1974).

These theories all take a look at language from the outside and see it in terms of other aspects of behaviour. They all recognize, in one way or another, two important functions of language: that it is 'about something' and so has an ideational function, and that it 'does something' socially, that it happens between and amongst people, and so has an inter-personal function. Linguists, particularly those of the Prague School (cf. Daneš (ed.), in press), who look at language 'from the inside' as well, also recognize that it has ways of 'doing its own thing', what has been called functional sentence perspective, or the textual function of language, which systematically relates the ideational and the inter-personal functions to linguistic structure, enabling language to meet the demands made on it by human experience and social intercourse (Halliday, 1967, 1969, 1973, 1975b). As regards language variation, field of discourse can be seen to be related mostly to the ideational function of language, personal and functional tenors to the inter-personal, and mode to the textual.

We have said (in Chapter one) that field of discourse is the linguistic reflection of the purposive role of the language user in the situation in which text has occurred (cf. Gregory, 1967, pp. 186–8). Another, not incompatible, way of putting it, from a more abstract and semantic point of view which sub- sumes some of what the present authors call functional tenor, is Halliday's (forthcoming): that 'field determines the selection of experiential [ideational] meanings, what socially recognized action the participants are engaged in, in which the exchange of verbal meanings has a part'. Gardiner (1932) pointed out that in speech events participants are revealing 'an intelligible purpose'; the language they use will reflect their desire to make sense, and this 'making sense' is in terms of the social activity they are engaged in, what is going on, and this may involve other 'goings on' that are not a part of the immediate situation.

If what is going on is the establishment or re-establishment of personal contact (phatic communion) the text in British English is likely to reflect such topics as 'the weather', 'the personal well-being of the participants' (usually not to be pursued in depth), 'the news' (national and/or local) or 'the cricket score'. In Nigerian English initial inquiries about 'the family' are highly probable. The following is a reasonably typical, if succinct, example of an interchange recorded between two professorial colleagues passing each other in the corridor of a Canadian university.

A: Hi, how are things?
B: Not so bad, and you?
A: Could be worse.
B: Hear the Budget?
A: Wish I hadn't.
B: (*Laugh*) Never mind, it's going to be a good weekend.
A: It had better be.
(*They continue on their way*)

Personal letters between friends are also characterized by topic switches and occasionally by exophoric references that sometimes make it difficult for a third person to understand fully what is going on. Idiolect may also be strongly marked, as in the following:

Darlings,
    Two lovely girls and ditto letters just arrived. I'll answer more properly in a day or two. The plane was only 5 mins. late and they were through customs in $\frac{1}{2}$ hour. We were in Bury by 11.30. I thought my two girls were half dead. But it seems I was wrong. They've gone Down Town Bury for the second time! We are now hoping a charitable organization called Corporation of Sons of Clergy will buy us a desirable residence just round the corner from here and rent it to us at £300 p.a. I'll know more when Dodds gets back this evening, and will write at length later. Edward, Liz and Charlotte (Liz's youngest sister) come this Thursday and will take the girls about a bit. I shall be ringing up Fanny and George to find out (a) whether they are home and (b) whether they would be willing to see Adam and three beauties. No. 3 being Carolanne Shaw who kindly lent her car for this occasion!
I must post this.
Tons & tons of love
Mummy

Both the texts quoted cover several topics but they both have enough cohesion for us to want to see them as each having one field of discourse. Field of discourse need not then be equated with topic or subject matter although they are instances of its manifestation. In texts of situations where language is very much subordinate and related to what is going on non-verbally, as, for example, the remarks made to each other by players during a game, or by two furniture removers attempting to get a grand piano up a staircase, there is likely to be a more direct and one-to-one action/topic/field of discourse relationship. Likewise in texts of situations in which language is virtually the whole of the meaningful action, as in a college seminar on the French Revolution, there tends to be a textually realized consistency of topic: another set of actions, those of the actual French Revolution, providing the basis of the 'subject matter' that is being verbalized. Fields of discourse such as gossip, reflection on the day or the week, etc., and general conversation, tend to be the ones in which there are shifts of topic and subject matter, a sequence of topics, each of which could be the realization of a dominant field of discourse but which in these instances are best thought of as indications of the non-restricted, non-specialist nature of the field of the particular text.

In Chapter one a distinction was suggested between technical (i.e. specialist) and non-technical fields. Many specialist roles in our society so restrict the language used to realize them verbally that they become fully comprehensible only to those acquainted with that specialization and its characteristic verbalized actions. In English, contrary to some popular opinion, this restricted nature of Technical English does not exclude them from being a part of Standard English; the criterion of 'high range of intelligibility' can be qualified as 'high range of intelligibility *among users acquainted with the field of discourse*'. The specialized English of Economics is used with mutual understanding by British, Canadian, American, Australian, African and Indian economists, and many others besides.

Specialist activities such as 'scientific and learned inquiry, administration, or professional pursuits and amateur enthusiasms' (Gregory, 1969, p. 3) lie behind such restricted languages. These technical fields have their own special vocabulary and favourite grammatical patterns. Lexically they tend to employ items proper only to themselves (e.g. molecule and neutron in the English of Physics; phoneme, morpheme and allophone in the English of Linguistics) as well as items common to the language as a whole but with their meaning specified through regular co-occurrence with other items (i.e. a restricted collocational range). The habitual collocation of voice with active and passive; mood with declarative, imperative and interrogative; and subject with predicator, adjunct and complement, distinguishes these three items in the English of Linguistics from that 'voice' that is 'raised', the 'mood' that can be 'bad' or 'good' and the 'subject' of a 'discussion'. Force, mass and energy in the English of Physics have predictable collocates (including each other) which distinguish them from the 'force' that collocates with 'police' or 'third', the 'mass' that collocates with 'riot', and the 'energy' of Phyllosan or Geritol advertisements.

Grammatically, the higher incidence of passive verbal groups in scientific fields of English than elsewhere in the language has often been noted. Many descriptive scientific fields also have characteristic and repetitive patterns of pre- and post-modification of nominal head words, as in the following:

From the English of Linguistics
(a) *clause*
   independent clause
   dependent clause
   nominal dependent clause
   nominal dependent clause operating as subject
   nominal dependent clause operating as subject in the
   independent clause
(from Gregory, 1972)

(b) verbal groups: *would live*

| SYSTEMIC DESCRIPTION | verbal group : (hypototactic/expansion) |

| STRUCTURAL DESCRIPTION | B: Modifier ◄ — —α : Head |

(from Halliday, forthcoming)

From the English of Anatomy (*Neurology*)
(a) *GVE fibers*
   sympathetic GVE fibers
   preganglionic sympathetic GVE fibers
   postganglionic sympathetic GVE fibers
   preganglionic parasympathetic fibers
   the ciliary ganglion and organs of the digestive,
      respiratory and urogenital systems

(b) *The cranial nerves*

Name	Functional Components	Deep Origin	Distribution
I Olfactory	Special visceral afferent	Olfactory mucous membrane	Olfactory mucous membrane
II Optic	Special somatic afferent	Retina (ganglion cells)	Retina
III Oculomotor	Somatic efferent	Oculomotor nucleus (mid-brain)	Extrinsic muscles of eye except superior oblique and lateral rectus

(from Edwards and Gaughram, 1971)

The nominal modification patterns of the (a) examples are related to the need in specialist activities for definition and precision as economically and unambiguously as possible, and the 'box' presentation of the (b) examples are related to the need for clear summary assignment and listing of features. It will be noted that there are indexical markers of these specialist fields at the levels of lexis and graphology as well as grammar. The graphological layout of the (b) examples is also an indexical marker of the functional tenor: expository (see Chapter five)—the same linguistic feature can be a marker of more than one dimension of variety; in other words, it can be multivalent. This text, from the field of discourse of the Christian religion, is revealing from this point of view:

The Twentieth Sunday After Trinity
The Collect

O ALMIGHTY and most merciful God, of thy bountiful goodness keep us, we beseech thee, from all things that may hurt us; that we, being ready both in body and soul, may cheerfully accomplish those things that thou wouldest have done; through Jesus Christ our Lord. *Amen.*

The lexical mutuality and grammatical modification and conjunction patterns of 'Almighty', 'most merciful', and 'God'; 'bountiful' and 'goodness'; 'body' and 'soul'; 'Jesus' and 'Christ' and 'Our Lord', mark the text as belonging to the field of discourse: Christian religion. The vocative element introduced by 'O', the particular use of colons and commas, and the italicized '*Amen*' (as an indication of a response by other speakers) can be taken as mode markers that this text is written to be spoken. The lexical items 'keep', 'beseech', the formulaic 'through Jesus Christ our Lord. *Amen*'; the initial vocative element; the imperative grammatical role of 'keep'; the modals 'may' and 'wouldest', are markers of the functional tenor of prayer. Together with the archaisms of 'thy', 'thee' and 'wouldest', and the respect-giving attributes 'Almighty and most merciful ... bountiful goodness', 'may', 'wouldest', 'beseech', 'Jesus Christ our Lord', are also markers of a formal personal tenor. Such a configuration of field, mode and tenors indicates a register of the Christian Collect. This can be regarded as a field-determined register, as the choices of mode and tenor can be seen as being consequentially related to the nature of the field of discourse.

Most scientific Englishes are also field-determined. The activity of science is a recording activity which means that it is committed to the written mode; and it has its own conventions of impersonality of presentation which means that there are few variations as regards tenors of discourse. Scientific texts tend to be expository in their functional addressee relationship and of mid-formality in their personal addressee relationship.

To the non-initiated reader, texts from specialist fields often seem impenetrable and unintelligible and so are frequently the object of ill-informed criticism, and are charged with being unnecessary jargons. However, it must be remembered that they are no new thing—a glance at the mathematics and philosophy of Ancient Greece and the theology of the twelfth and thirteenth centuries indicates that they have always been a necessary part of specialist communication and they are likely to be more ubiquitous in an epoch of rapid scientific and technological development such as ours.

A specialized language can, of course, be misused and become a mask concealing what is really being said or the fact that there is nothing very much being said. There are also sets of language habits among English users today which are somewhat spuriously specialist 'jargons'. A telling indictment of such pseudo-specialist Englishes is made in George Orwell's famous essay 'Politics and the English Language' (1945):

> Consider for example some comfortable English professor defending Russian totalitarianism. He cannot say outright, 'I believe in killing off your opponents when you can get good results by doing so.' Probably, therefore, he will say something like this:
>
> 'While freely conceding that the Soviet regime exhibits certain features which the humanitarian may be inclined to deplore, we must, I think, agree that a certain curtailment of the right to political opposition is an unavoidable concomitant of transitional periods, and that the rigors which the Russian people have been called upon to undergo have been amply justified in the sphere of concrete achievement.'

Another famous novelist, Aldous Huxley, made a similar criticism in his essay 'The Language of War' (1937) and he put his finger on the psychological roots of such texts: 'The language we use about war is inappropriate, and its inappropriateness is designed to conceal a reality so odious that we do not wish to know it.' What is involved here is not the use of a precise specialist language to communicate specialist analysis but the use of euphemism to conceal the real nature of the experience that is being verbalized. So 'to assassinate' becomes 'to terminate with extreme prejudice' and in his essay Orwell deals trenchantly with the 'real meaning' of 'pacification', 'transfer of population' and 'rectification of frontiers'. The involvement of the USA in Vietnam has added a host more to English. We must, however, be careful not to become too indignant about this aspect of language behaviour. Euphemisms are a continuing feature of language and they fulfil a healthy function when they help to make the genuinely intolerable, tolerable; they can, of course, help us tolerate that which should not be tolerated. And sometimes they can just be funny: as in Alan Herbert's translation into 'officialese' of Nelson's famous signal to the English fleet at Trafalgar—England expects that every man will do his duty—as 'England anticipates that with regard to the current emergency, personnel will duly implement their obligations in accordance with the functions allocated to their respective age groups.'

Very different from what we have just been discussing is the kind of specialized English which involves communicating succinctly and directly to those who know or are expected to be able to learn the field of activity being verbalized. As has been noted these are not confined to the scholar and the scientist. Recipe books, knitting and sewing patterns, car manuals, fashion and gun magazines, both reflect and answer to the needs of professional and amateur cooks, dress-makers, mechanics and sportsmen.

Such specialized fields often show in one language the influence of another whose culture has been in the vanguard of the activity being verbalized. Many French items are in the English of Cookery, Italian in the English of Music, and elements of English are frequent in many languages when soccer, science and technology are the fields of discourse.

Specialized fields of discourse can, of course, be more or less restricted in communicability to those who already know a great deal about what is being presented linguistically; and often what they are as pieces of language, particularly as regards their texture, is the consequence not only of their fields of discourse but also of their associated modes and tenors of discourse. What an actual text really is results from the configuration of all the dimensions of diatypic variation (see Chapter six).

Similarly, although it is useful to see field of discourse as related to the experiential function of language, the choice of what 'field' is used in a given situation can be connected to the relationship between the language users present in that situation, and so have ramifications as regards the inter-personal function of language—and specialized fields in particular have consequences as regards the textual function of language. Specialized texts are more endophorically cohesive, i.e. they hang together by internal reference; they can stand by themselves as pieces of language, and, like literary texts, do not need an awareness of the immediate situation of their occurrence for full understanding. The 'personal-contact' and 'gossip' fields discussed at the beginning of this chapter, on the other hand, often produce texts that are fully understandable only by the immediate participants in the language event in the light of their shared knowledge. They often work by exophoric reference (reference outside of the text) and are characteristic of the spoken mode: specialized fields are characteristically 'at home', as it were, in the written mode.

Chapter four

Modes of discourse

'Oh, I can't stand him, he talks like a book.'

'He's a good talker but he's hopeless when he tries to put it down on paper.'

In order to understand and keep in perspective the concept of mode of discourse it is necessary to be clear about the distinction that can be made between language and medium. Abercrombie (1967, pp. 1–2) lucidly illustrates this important distinction:

> If we compare a piece of written English with a piece of spoken English, regarding them simply as physical objects or events and forgetting for the moment the fact that they convey meaning to us, it is apparent at once that they bear no resemblance to each other whatever. The piece of written English consists of groups of small black marks arranged on a white surface, while the piece of spoken English consists of a succession of constantly varying noises. It would hardly be possible for two things to be more different. However, we have only to recall the fact that both of them convey meaning, to be in no doubt that, utterly dissimilar as they may be, they are both equally English. As soon as we make explicit this identity lying behind the complete difference, we have in fact drawn the distinction in question: we have recognized, in effect, that the piece of spoken English and the piece of written English are the same *language* embodied in different *mediums*, one medium consisting of shapes, the other of noises.
> It is possible for the same language to be conveyed by different mediums because the language itself lies in the

patterns which the mediums form, and not in the physical objects or events, as such, of which the mediums consist. When we distinguish language from medium, what we are doing is to distinguish a pattern from its material embodiment, of which, in a sense, it is independent. Language, we could say, is *form*, while the medium is substance.

Granted this distinction, it is still crucial to recognize that the same language has the possibility of variation in the patterns and kinds of patterns that occur according to which medium is embodying it. We can recognize people who 'talk like a book' as well as people who write 'like they talk'; and only a little reflection leads us to realize that there are things we can do when we are talking (e.g. express by vocal features irony, sarcasm, rage, amatory interests) which we have to find a different way of expressing when we are writing, and *vice versa* (which raises the question as to whether there are phonological equivalents of the paragraph, italics, quotation marks, etc.). So differences in medium can yield variations within the same language. Situationally what is involved here is the users' medium relationship; the distinctive set of linguistic features associated with a particular, recurring relationship constitutes a contextual mode of discourse.

Initially, of course, the relationship of a user to his medium may be seen as the simple one of which he is using—speech or writing. But 'as soon as relationships such as those between lectures and articles, between conversations in real life and dialogue in novels and plays, have to be considered, distinctions amongst modes of discourse, if they are to be really useful, have often to be more delicate than the primary one between spoken and written' (Gregory, 1967, p. 188). What follows are some suggested distinctions first made by Gregory (*op. cit.*) and used by Benson and Greaves (1973).

If we examine the situations in which people speak rather than write we can distinguish between those in which they are speaking spontaneously as opposed to those in which they are speaking non-spontaneously (as the actor and the lecturer

most often are doing); and within spontaneous speech an
important distinction may be made between conversing and
monologuing. Conversing has been described (Gregory, *op.
cit.*, p. 188) as 'the medium relationship in which there is a
possibility of spontaneous interchange between two or more
people' and Abercrombie (1963a) has pointed out that although
most language is the result of such activity, we do not know as
much about it as we do about other modes of language which
traditionally, and quite naturally, are more permanently
recorded for study. The advent of, and then improvements in,
the tape-recorder, particularly its reduction in size and obtrus-
iveness through solid-state engineering, has increased, over
the last fifteen years, our ability to study texts that arise from
the activity of conversing. Quirk (1955) has commented on the
incidence in conversation of what he calls 'intimacy signals',
and Abercrombie (1963a) on what he calls 'silence fillers',
phrases like 'sort of', kind of', 'you know', 'I mean to say',
and has noted that intonational rather than pausal features
frequently mark the end of sentences. One also observes
'sentence-sharing' or completion between speakers, as in:

A: Are you going to?
B: Go to the dance? Yes.

Most existing grammars of English are based on the observation of written language, or the speaking of what is written,
and so the grammar of conversation often appears to have a
kind of incompleteness:

1. Going to buy one?
2. Don't know. Perhaps.
3. Better hurry, they're packing up.
4. Oh, all right.
5. That one over there, please, the big one.

Noticeable in this interchange is the apparent omission of
grammatical subject (sentences 1 and 2, first clause in sentence
3, sentence 4), auxiliary verb (sentence 1 and first clause in
sentence 3), any verb at all (sentences 4 and 5), the absence of
substantives and the use of substitution items like 'one',

'they', and pointing items like 'That' and 'over there'. Even as it stands, however, the text 'makes sense' and 'means' something, and given situational information, such as that this text was recorded at a pumpkin stall towards the end of the day at a Canadian fall fair, it makes even more 'sense'. This information, of course, was shared by the speakers, was part of the meaning of their saying; they knew who each other was, where they were, and who 'they' were, and what 'it' was, and so the omissions are, in a sense, apparent rather than real. There is no problem if we consider it to be language as a kind of doing.

Monologuing is taken to be the users' medium relationship in those speech situations in which the other people present, if any, do not join in, or at least are not meant to, except perhaps to show approval or disapproval. Benson and Greaves (*op. cit.*, p. 82) contrast monologuing and conversing as follows:

> *Monologuing* is the speaking by one individual in such a way as to exclude the possibility of interruption by others. *Conversing* is speaking in such a way as to invite the participation of others. It is quite possible for one person to converse at another and be the only speaker; he need only ask a series of genuine questions, for example, without receiving an answer. Similarly two people can monologue at each other. Try listening to a conversation between crashing bores at a social gathering for an example of this phenomenon.

The types of speech situation which lead to this kind of sustained spontaneous speech include classroom teaching, television and radio interviews (particularly if the person being interviewed is in a highly verbal profession), sporting commentaries on radio and television of an event actually taking place, and what are often mistaken to be conversations between experts in a particular field and which are in fact exchanges of monologues. There is, of course, a cline of more-to-less spontaneity in this particular medium relationship. The sporting commentator has studied notes and has described this sort of thing before; and people whose professions are highly verbal ones, such as the journalist, the politician, the preacher, the teacher, the lawyer and the stage entertainer, become accustomed to monologuing, and are very often called upon to speak spontaneously about the same area of experience. This means that although they have no written text in front of them there are elements of preparation and repetition in their speaking performances which give them some of the characteristics of written modes.

Monologue texts are characterized by more phonological, grammatical and lexical cohesion (see Chapter eight and Halliday and Hasan, 1976) than many conversational texts: pronouns and demonstratives are more likely to have an intra-textual referent. There is about them a considerable amount of linguistically realized completeness. They often rely less than conversation on shared experience between speaker and hearer(s), or on features of the immediately and perceptually present situation. The situation created by the language itself tends to be more important than the extra-linguistic situation. This means that monologue usually has more apparent continuity and self-containedness than much conversation. It would seem that monologue is very much a mode of the educated speaker who has what Coleridge called a 'sense of prospective', an idea of what has been said, what is going to be said, and their relationship to what is being said at the moment. Our observations of the spontaneous speech of not so well educated speakers have indicated that it is usually only when the language event becomes anecdotal in character (such as 'hospital stories', 'what happened at the dance', extended gossip about other people not present) that there are likely to be the indexical markers of monologue: sustained, cohesive speech by one person.

The habitual use of, and control of, the sub-mode of monologue can be seen, then, to be a potential marker of a speaker's idiolect, whether that speaker is a highly articulate television pundit or an old lady that 'runs off at the mouth', and the content and nature of the speaker's monologuing can be related to the elaborated/restricted code distinction (see Chapter seven). Elaborated code users tend to be accustomed to using language to create experience beyond the immediate present and so seem to have a greater variety of monologuing capacities than do restricted code users for whom anecdote, the re-telling of a past experience, appears to be the main occasion for monologuing.

Non-spontaneous speech may be sub-categorized either as reciting or as the speaking of what is written. Reciting as a technical term refers to the medium relationship that is involved in the telling of stories, the recitation of poems and the singing of songs that belong to an oral tradition and do not have a written version behind them. This mode of language is a major one in non-literate societies. In a culture such as ours it is usually manifested in certain varieties of children's language (usually associated with games) and in jokes and lyrics of the kind that used to be described as 'doubtful'.

In literate cultures most non-spontaneous speech is the speaking of what has been written. The text which has been written may be written to be spoken as if not written (e.g. play texts), or written to be spoken (e.g. many political speeches and lectures) with no such conventional pretence, or even written not necessarily to be spoken (as, for example, are both telephone directories and novels). This sub-categorization of writing in terms of the kind and degree of its orientation towards the spoken mode needs, perhaps, some justification. In the linguistic development of both the individual and the community, speech precedes writing. There are languages that are spoken and not written but every written language is spoken. Most of us 'speak' what we write when we are writing. Furthermore, in complex media-conscious societies an increasing proportion of language is written with the speaking of it definitely in mind.

When the actor performs, having learnt his lines and rehearsed them, he is speaking what is written to be spoken as if not written. The text he produces is one text; the text of the play another, which is written to be spoken as if not written.

This mode of speech is most often found in performance of plays and in films, radio and television. On occasions some apparently spontaneous political speeches, sermons and lectures belong to this mode. It has many markers similar to spontaneous speech but it is not, of course, identical with it, as both T. S. Eliot (1959), from the writer's point of view, and Abercrombie (1963a), from the linguist's, have indicated. If the actor on the stage spoke as people do in 'real life', with frequent *non sequiturs*, false starts, allusions, digressions, sentence fragments, etc., two things would be likely to happen: the audience would suspect that the actor had failed to learn his lines; and, more importantly, perhaps, the audience would be unlikely to be getting the information it needs to get, in order that the 'two-hours' traffic of the stage' emerges as a whole and understandable experience. Great playwrights, such as Shakespeare, Shaw or Pinter, for example, give the effect of spontaneous speech rather than the reality of it. Written and spoken texts of these related modes are usually distinguished linguistically from other written texts because they make more use of the favourite grammatical patterns of spontaneous speech such as elision, exclamatory units and 'tag' repetitions like 'You know that, don't you'. On the other hand they differ from texts of spontaneous speech because they tend to make less frequent use of pronouns and demonstratives without intra-textual referents and appear to be 'fuller' linguistically because they use language to create their situations to a greater extent than people do when engaged in spontaneous speech.

> The fundamental difference between the *speaking* of what is written to be spoken as if not written and ordinary speech is that the one is planned, prepared behaviour, the other spontaneous; a play or film largely creates its own situation and patterns of contextual relations, has a definite beginning and end, and is remarkably and significantly more compact and self-contained than the situations in which conversing and monologuing occur (Gregory, 1967, p. 192).

The scripts for most political speeches, sermons, lectures and academic papers, and all news bulletins and commentaries on the news on radio and television are also written with their vocal delivery in mind, but there is not usually any effort made to conceal the written origin of the spoken text. Such texts may be characterized as written to be spoken. Those that are of some length tend to contain, quite deliberately, a large amount of varied repetition. Most texts of this kind are spoken in situations in which the hearer is not in the reader's position of being able to 'turn back a page' to check if he understood something in the earlier part of the text or to link two parts of the text. Effective texts written to be spoken recognize this fact, and their authors are aware that speech activity of this kind is usually an irreversible sequence of vocal behaviour and so help the hearer by making the main points over again in a slightly different way, so that the text does not seem too repetitive at the same time as it keeps its main messages in the hearers' minds. Those sermons, speeches and lectures which are really the reading aloud of an article or essay are often unsatisfactory because they lack consciousness of the differences in mode demands between that which is to be read with the eye and that which is to be heard with the ear. News bulletins, which have other constraints upon them, such as shortness of time, tend to solve this problem by 'headlines' at the beginning, and a repetition of main items of news at the end of the broadcast.

Special cases of texts written to be spoken are liturgical prayers and poetry. The former have their own distinctive kind of varied repetition relating to their field of discourse and functional tenors (praise, confession, petition, credal assertion, thanksgiving, etc.) as well as their mode (cf. Gregory, *op. cit.*, p. 193), and in the criticism of poetry it is important to recognize that although all written poetic texts have some essential phonic implications, e.g. rhyme, alliteration, assonance, metre, homophonic ambiguity, they do also remain written texts that exist in their own right and can also make significant use of the resources of the written language, e.g. paragraphing, the graphic line, italics, capitalization, homographic ambiguities (cf. Levin, 1962). The present authors cannot, however, completely agree with Halliday (1973, 1975b) whose more abstract use of the term mode as the 'rhetorical channel' (seeming to subsume within it what is here dealt with as functional tenor) leads him to assign most considerations of *genre* to this particular dimension. We prefer to characterize *genre* in terms of all the dimensions of language variety. Most significant literary *genres*, such as epic, ode, lyric, sonnet, tragedy, farce and comedy, have author/reader expectations as regards not only the medium relationship involved but also as regards the purposive roles/on-going social activities, and the personal and functional addressee relationships which are at risk, and so field and personal and functional tenors are likewise relevant to their description. Literary *genres* can be seen as individual kinds of marked register within literature.

Since the growth and spread of literacy there has been a great amount of language written not necessarily to be spoken, and until recently it was this part of the language which was studied as language in schools and universities. Benson and Greaves (*op. cit.*, p. 83) comment succinctly on the major sub-modes of this sort of written language, as follows:

> There remains language *written not necessarily to be spoken*. Such language may bear no appreciable relation to the spoken mode; for example the telephone book . . . or a dictionary. Such language is more delicately described as *written to be read*.

> Language may be written not necessarily to be spoken, but with a relationship to the spoken mode; for example, the dialogue in a novel, *to be read as speech* [cf. *to be read as if heard*, Gregory, *op. cit.*, p. 193].

> Related to this, because it implies a person 'making' the language, is the interior monologue, *to be read as if thought* [cf. *to be read as if overheard*, Gregory, *ibid.*].

However, the orientation of so much written language to its potential vocalization, or, at least, to the possibility of an auditory experience—witness the conventions of direct speech (see Gregory, 1965), the indications of ways of speaking such as 'he murmured softly', 'she yelped', 'he joked', etc., the marked and recurrent devices of a Joycean monologue (see Spencer, 1965)—should not obscure the fact that written

language has its own medium resources: paragraphing, italiciz-
ation, change of type, quotations marks, etc., that have no
clear analogue in the spoken mode. A text such as this one,
found on a bottle of single malt whisky,

is very much a written text.

As field is largely related to the ideational function of
language, and personal and functional tenors to the inter-
personal, so mode can be seen as related primarily to the
textual, the enabling function (Halliday, forthcoming):

> The selection of options in the textual systems, such as
> those of theme [concerned with the user's point of
> departure in a sentence], information [concerned with
> what is new and what is given] and voice [passive or
> active], and also the selection of cohesive patterns, those
> of reference, substitution and ellipsis, and conjunction,
> tend to be determined by the symbolic forms taken by
> the interaction, in particular the place that is assigned to
> the text in the total situation. This includes the
> distinction of medium, written or spoken, and the complex
> sub-varieties derived from these.

However, mode and the choice of mode have relations also
with the ideational function by way of field of discourse: there
are those things we tend to talk about, and those we tend to
write about. There are also relations with language's inter-
personal function by way of personal and functional tenors:
formal and written tend to go together as do informal and
spoken, and the phatic function is common in the spoken
mode as is the descriptive in the written. In spoken English

there are also important phonological systems known as 'key' systems (cf. Halliday, forthcoming) which, for example, can indicate what sort of question, command or statement is being made; and this, of course, is central to the inter-personal function of language. Nevertheless it must be remembered that a reader is also a speaker even if he is speaking to himself, and such systems are not altogether inaccessible to the reader of the written mode as he sub-vocalizes it to himself in terms of the co-text and the context of the piece. As was noted at the beginning of this chapter, the mediums may be distinct but they realize the same language; however, they do so in a way that gives rise to complex and important sub-varieties.

Figure 1

Suggested distinctions along the dimension of situation variation categorized as user's medium relationship

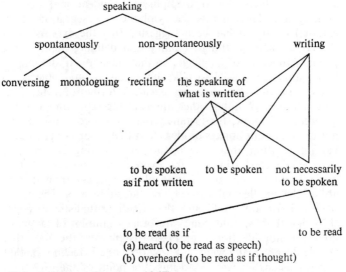

(Adapted from Gregory, 1967)

Chapter five

Tenors of discourse

'What are you trying to tell me?'

'Don't speak to me like that—I'm your mother.'

A social theory of language gives primacy to the role that language plays linking people together in various kinds of social interaction; defining relative statuses and personalities; establishing, maintaining or ending relationships. That language is used (and not used) in an inter-personal function has relevance to both a formal descriptive analysis of language and a general understanding of language activity.

Many treatments of language, particularly discussions of semantics and logic, tend to emphasize the ideational function of language: language as the symbolic representation of an external reality. It has been suggested that the expression of the relationship of things, naming and defining them, is the primary function of language, so that, in popular thought at least, language is used to talk about persons and objects, to impart information, to communicate information, etc. That language may be doing other things at the same time is often ignored. We know, for instance, that language is often used not to talk about objects or ideas 'out there' but rather to convey information about the relationship existing between the two people conversing: so the expression 'You swine!' tells more about the emotional state of the speaker than it does about the intellectual capacity of the addressee. The ritual 'Hello. How are you?' and the equally ritualistic response 'Just fine thanks. And you?' are other examples of language used for non-ideational purposes. Deploring the fact that people do not really want to know how one is feeling, or that nobody listens anyway, is to miss the point of the exchange. Greetings are given to people that one knows and wants to (or must) recognize (cf. Appendix). Not to recognize the relationship would be to change it or even possibly end it. We thus continue to ask people how they are, replying that we are fine too, without giving much thought to what we are saying. Such is the nature of the ritual.

Any study of language-in-use must not underestimate the importance of social and expressive functions of language in comparison to its 'cognitive' functions. The term 'cognitive' is itself ill-chosen since it implies that the recognition of social roles and relationships is somehow less important than the recognition of physical objects or the apprehension of ideas. The smooth interaction of individuals depends upon their learning and accepting rules of social behaviour. And along with learning roles we have to learn how to identify role-markers which are both linguistic and non-linguistic. We learn how to identify relationships, how to establish, alter and end them. This knowledge is a normal and necessary part of man's social behaviour.

The misrepresentation of the importance of the social aspect of linguistic behaviour is, however, quite common. The interest in language as sound-symbol representing object-thing or person-thing has overshadowed the fact that language can and does represent the dynamics of human interaction as well. The fact that a certain individual possesses a certain rank in an organization entitles him to be addressed in a certain fashion by his subordinates, in another way by his equals, and in a third manner by his superiors. Similarly, speaking the 'right' kind of language may mean inclusion in a group while, conversely, speaking the 'wrong' kind almost automatically means exclusion. 'It's not what you said, it's how you said it'—certainly there is some truth in this common remark. Language shapes relationships, it defines and identifies them. It can bring people closer together, or it can separate them. These very important functions of language are purely social in nature.

To come to terms with how roles and relationships are realized in language, we speak of tenors of discourse. Tenor reflects how the addresser (the speaker or the writer) interacts with the addressee (the listener or the reader) in an addressee relationship. The addressee relationship is the situational category, the extra-linguistic reality which is shown through the contextual category of tenor (see Chapter one).

The exact nature of the addressee relationship depends upon divisions of social structure; on the way in which any society is organized. It is social structure which determines the number and types of roles we can play, either in relation to sociological attributes (class features) or personal attributes (aspects of personal relationships). These divisions may be determined by economic variables (such as salary, earned or unearned wealth), by education ('the Harvard man' has linguistic recognition. Does anyone speak of 'the Alabama State man'?), by profession, by sex, and so on. Societies differ in that the divisions are not the same; nor are the same values attributed to the same categories. More importance is given to ascribed characteristics in traditional societies than is habitually given in Western societies.

Every individual who belongs to a given society will fit in some of the categories, and his status within the community will depend upon the groups that he can claim membership in. The person who has legal training, practises law, belongs to a society of barristers and solicitors, *is* a lawyer just as that person may be at the same time a man or woman, a father or a mother, a tennis player or a golfer, an apartment dweller or a homeowner, an *habitué* of the theatre or a stay-at-home. The person will be defined in terms of categories like these and there will be an appropriate code of behaviour both linguistic and non-linguistic for each of these identities. From the linguistic perspective, the individual's speech patterns will be determined and shaped by his previous experiences. A lawyer will talk like a lawyer about legal matters. A mother will talk like a mother to her children or about her children. The language is simply one aspect of the total pattern of behaviour consonant with the role. Furthermore the language the individual uses will re-define each situation. A first meeting between individuals may show each as defining the relationship as that of stranger to stranger. Later meetings will show variations in the actions and language of the participants.

Changes in the status of the participants will most certainly be shown verbally.

Verbal changes frequently signal an overt attempt to alter the relationship. The attempt may then be verbally acknowledged and accepted, or rebuked. The cocktail-party conversation provides ample illustration of the ways in which language is used to further or to impede a personal relationship:

'Well, did you ask her to dinner?'

'Yes.'

'Well, what did she say?'

'She said that without her sun glasses I really wasn't her type.'

In this way, through language, we learn our roles. We learn about our social status, about relationships between different kinds of people (see Chapter seven). We learn about appropriate kinds of occupational behaviour at the same time as we acquire technical information (the professional code of ethics merely makes this explicit). We learn how to behave with different individuals with every new encounter. We learn what to do and what to say. We learn, too, how to say it.

At the semantic level tenor realizes the inter-personal function of language (Halliday, 1973, 1975a, 1975b). Tenor can express the degree of formality of the relationship—the personal tenor of that relationship—or it may reflect the role that language is playing in the situation—the functional tenor of the relationship. The degree of familiarity or formality can be expressed non-verbally often through the degree and kind of physical contact permitted between people (Goffman, 1963, 1971). Wives are usually kissed on the lips (in some Western societies at least), maiden aunts on the cheek, children on the forehead or cheek, the pope on his ring. The conversation between a husband and wife shows markers of intimacy and informality whether the situation be an amorous *tête-à-tête* or a full-scale battle. Much of what is said relates in an important way to what is not said. It has been suggested that there is an inverse relationship between the degree of formality existing between people and the need to make information verbally explicit (Joos, 1962); the more knowledge two people share, the less they need to talk about it. Elliptical reference, abbreviations, even non-verbal signals, permit a considerable conservation of energy. They also allow people to talk openly about things they otherwise would not want to. Note, for example, the various code words between children and parents to refer to natural bodily functions. At the same time that direct reference to situation can be avoided, much will be said between intimates that goes beyond the immediate environment. The language used will communicate about the nature of an on-going relationship. So the announcement that reads 'L'essentiel est invisible pour les yeux. On ne voit bien qu'avec le cœur. St-Exupéry' has really nothing at all to do with French literature, and can only be understood by the addresser and the addressee. The significant situation in this instance is not defined at all in terms of physical environment or temporal event. The significant situation *is* the relationship of addresser to addressee.

The relationship of the after-dinner speaker to his audience, or of the Queen in her annual end-of-the-year Commonwealth address, is revealed as one of formality by markers like, 'Mr Chairman, Honourable delegates, Ladies and Gentlemen', or 'My fellow Countrymen', or even 'To my most loyal subjects'. These greetings indicate immediately the roles to be played by both the addresser and the addressee. Address systems are perhaps the most obvious means of indicating roles and relationships. They include title, rank and kinship terminology and sex. It is perhaps for this reason that writing letters these days can sometimes be tiresome if the sex of the addressee is not known. If 'Dear Sir' is no longer acceptable ('Gentlemen' is even worse) do we dare write 'To whom it may concern'? That still seems somewhat rude although less absurd than 'Dear Person'. If ours were 'a classless society' we could neatly sidestep the problem by referring to everyone as 'Comrade'. However, ranks and titles are often won with difficulty and we cling to them. It is interesting to note, in this regard, the changing use, in Canada, of Dr and name with reference to PhDs. The greater the number of doctorates the more the use of title seems to be an affectation. Even in academic circles the use is restricted to formal situations or to very highly respected individuals (the age factor sometimes plays a role here). In the meantime we can only hope that the etiquette books will be revised.

Functional tenor is the category used to describe what language is being used for in the situation. Is the speaker trying to persuade? to exhort? to discipline? Language can be used for these purposes and many others. The addresser can select from a number of different lines of functional tenor to determine the exact nature of the functional relationship. Functional tenor differs markedly, therefore, from personal tenor which constitutes a single line ranging from highly informal to highly formal. With functional tenor it is normally only the positive end of the line that is interesting; if in a given text language is didactic it is this aspect that concerns us, not the fact that it is not amatory, not insulting, not persuasive, not expository.

The generic structure of text is often defined in terms of functional tenor. The tenor can be considered as the micro-function; the immediate use of the text in situation. An adver-tisement is by definition an attempt to persuade through both linguistic and visual means. The tenor of persuasion defines the generic structure of 'the ad', as the sermon is designed to exhort and to teach. The functional tenor may be more-or-less explicit. Advertising can be hard-sell or soft-sell. And it can appeal linguistically to a set of learned attitudes and prejudices, as may be illustrated by the following:

As most socially apt people know, poppycock is the nonsense spoken by other people and they produce it with practically no effort at all. On the other hand Poppycock is produced with considerable care, skill and judgement from hand-picked almonds, high-class pecans and popcorn chosen for its sense of humour. Butter, sugar and salt have been added to provide each bite with a delicious upper crust. Made in small batches to preserve its flavour, Poppycock should be passed around quickly among the best people.

The choice of a marker of social dialect and of formality like Poppycock, the product name, reveals the particular orientation of the advertisement (as do names like Brut, Vitalis, Tigress, etc.). The collocation of 'popcorn' and 'sense of humour', 'high-class' and 'pecans', 'salt', 'sugar' and 'butter' with 'upper crust', although unusual (thus lending to the humour in the advertisement) is perfectly in keeping with the personal tenor of the advertisement, and with the suggestion that because the product is known by the company it keeps it must be good since it is only seen in the 'best circles'.

Functional and personal tenors may be independent of one another. This is seen typically with certain functional tenors that can hit any point on the formality/familiarity scale. A university lecture can be a highly formal piece of language, read aloud from a written text, using formal greetings, many passive constructions and a technical vocabulary. But depending on the preferences of the lecturer, on the traditions of the university, the size of the class and the field of discourse, it might also be delivered quite spontaneously, in an ad-lib style with jokes or puns, personal anecdotes, references to students in the class, and other markers of informal discourse.

In a similar way the insult may be formal or informal, blunt and crude or elliptic and ironic. Compare the styles of insult in this passage from Hemingway's *Islands in the Stream* (1970, p. 30).

'Can't you filthy-mouthed swine let a lady sleep?' the man said. 'Why don't you just go down below,' Frank said to him. 'You're liable to get in trouble around here using all those epithets. You haven't got your chauffeur here to look after you. Does your chauffeur always take you to school?' 'He doesn't go to school, Frank,' Fred Wilson said, putting aside his guitar. 'He's a grown-up boy. He's a businessman. Can't you recognize a big businessman?' 'Are you a businessman, sonny?' Frank asked. 'Then you know it's good business for you to run along down into your cabin. There isn't any good business for you up here.' 'He's right,' Fred Wilson said.

'You haven't future around with us. Just go down to your
cabin. You'll get used to the noise.' 'You filthy swine,'
the man said and looked at them all.

The insulting epithet—'filthy swine'—is more direct but the
use of the address term 'sonny' and its sardonic collocation
with 'businessman', the reference to 'school', the contradictory
'grown-up boy', the equivocal use of 'business' in 'businessman' and 'it's good business for you to run along', mark the
rest of the dialogue too as insult. The difference is in the
degree of formality, between being not quite vulgar ('You
filthy swine' sounds almost like an insult past its prime,
somewhat like 'You cad') or merely familiar.

Tenor expresses the roles and statuses of the participants in
this scene. Their linguistic roles are not created in language;
rather they are created in the external, real-world environment.
We suggested that tenor reflects individual experience. Cumu-
lative experience will determine the linguistic expression of the
immediate situation and so a link can be made between tenor
and idiolect. The habitual expressions of the speaker will be
compatible with the social roles he can fill. The professional
teacher may more readily assume a didactic or expository
functional tenor outside of the teaching situation.

There seems, too, to be a direct relationship between personal experience and the ability to control and switch tenors.
The colourful profanity of the sailor, for example, is celebrated.
Most of us could not even attempt to use with flair the most
informal of the points on the personal-tenor cline. On the
other hand most of us could not master the most formal
degrees either as exemplified by the fine points of an old-style
grammarian or diction specialist. We tend generally to operate
in the middle ranges but the capacity to cover a wide or narrow
range at either end of the scale will be determined by what the
speaker has learned as being appropriate to the situation.

While all experience is ultimately unique, each of us as
members of the same society and culture shares similar
experiences, values and knowledge with other members,
although the interpretation of even the same event, or the

understanding that we have of an idea, remains highly individual. These similar experiences are enough to make us feel that we form a group with others, that we are more like group members than non-members. We define ourselves as partisans, and our language will reveal our partisanship. The language of a salesman will resemble that of other salesmen, just as people from the same region tend to sound the same; and just as personal experience contributes to the knowledge and control of different personal and functional tenors, so group experience contributes to the ways in which groups use tenors. If you are a wealthy Brahmin in India, you and all other wealthy Brahmins will expect to receive linguistic markers of respect from lower-caste members. You, on the other hand, will not be accustomed to giving those same markers to any but other Brahmins.

Similarly a salesman learns to try and persuade people with his 'pitch': as a part of his occupation and customary behaviour the salesman tends to become incorporated into his idiolect.

The relationship of tenor to idiolect poses special problems for the second-language learner. A student of another language brings to his learning task all of the habits, knowledge and attitudes of his mother tongue and his culture. Learning a second language involves suspending these, in many instances, often with great difficulty, and acquiring others. The student, however, will often continue to interpret situations as he would in his own culture (if they are not so utterly different as to be uninterpretable) and employ those tenors in the new language that are most like those he already knows. Unfortunately the understanding that there are rules of behaviour to acquire as well as rules of grammar has not been stressed by educators. While the student may leave the class knowing what to say, less often does he know when to say it and to whom. In other words, his grasp of tenors is incomplete. He may often have a formal tenor and perhaps a relatively informal one, but he may not know the gradations in between or the extremes. It seems somehow dishonest to suggest to the student, as is sometimes done, that there is an 'all-purpose', neutral tenor useful in all situations or even in the types of situations that the second-language learner will find himself in. The former does not exist and it is difficult to know how educators can predict the kinds of situations that the student will enter into.

The situation can be even more complicated if tenor is marked by shifts in dialect or language. Gumperz (1966, p. 179) cites the difficulties of Westerners who have learned Hindi in order to work and talk with native Indians only to discover that they will not be addressed in Hindi but rather in English. They become understandably upset and frustrated—they know how to speak, they want to but they cannot. To understand why not, one must know something about the nature of social relationships in India and how they are marked linguistically. It appears that the use of Hindi when addressing speakers of English is a marker of relatively informal or intimate status. Indians will tend to address Westerners who are strangers in English to mark personal distance. Only when the relationship has become less formal can the language use change. This type of situation then is comparable to the shift from 'Mr X' to 'Bob' in English, or the shift in German from 'Sie' to 'Du'. Only when the friendship has progressed can the shift be made from English to Hindi.

Since we find that groups tend to use language in similar ways because of similar experiences, we find that the use of tenor also relates to the use of code (see Chapter seven) as it does to idiolect, and to geographical, social and temporal dialects. Interpretations of situation, the way a group sees its position as regards itself and others, will determine the range of tenors it typically selects from. The selections will be made from those permanent characteristics available to the user as defined by dialect. In French, for example, one can use either 'tu' or 'vous' (singular) to address someone. The choice between them has depended historically on a number of factors. At one time 'vous' was used as a marker of social position, ascribed status. Servants addressed noblemen as 'vous', noblemen addressed servants with 'tu' regardless of the degree of familiarity in the relationship. Children called parents 'vous' while the latter used 'tu' to them. Social equals called each other either 'vous' or 'tu' depending on which class they belonged to. So usage marked social dialect. Changes, however, took place (making the first use a marker of temporal dialect) and gradually the use of 'tu' became a marker of familiarity and solidarity (Brown and Gilman, 1960), 'vous' became a marker of formality and respect. Children and parents called each other reciprocally 'tu'; husband and wife, and close friends all used the 'informal' 'tu', reserving 'vous' for use with strangers.

Lately, usage has changed again, at least in Canadian varieties of French. 'Tu' is used among young people even with strangers and recent acquaintances. While a young person may on occasion address an elderly person with the formal marker as a sign of respect, such a usage with people of his own generation would be immediately and mockingly commented upon. So again the shift marks the more conservative usage as a feature of a different temporal dialect.

Tenors in English vary, too, according to dialect. Regional dialects may vary from what seems the excessive politeness of some Indian English dialects to the excessively egalitarian North American varieties, and comedians make use of this range.

As noted in Chapter two, some fields of discourse are usually associated with specific tenors. In addition, tenor will vary with the mode used. A telephone call to the dentist may evoke a 'Good morning, Dr Jones's office', but a letter from the same would more typically begin 'Dear Mr Smith'. Involved here is a constant field of discourse 'dental business'; a constant personal tenor of moderate formality; mode variables between spoken/written, telephonic/epistolary; and functional tenor variables between responding/initiating. Because register is a configuration of certain expectancies involving field, mode and tenors, a business letter dealing with an overdue account is as predictable as regards tenor as field. So, too, the evening News begins 'Good evening' and ends with 'Good night'; and a sermon might begin 'My dear brothers and sisters in Christ' and end 'In the name of the Father, and of the Son and of the Holy Ghost'. Each of these instances of language use is identified in part by a constant association of a given personal and functional tenor and a specific recurring feature of situation. Personal tenor will also vary with mode. A spoken greeting may range from a quick 'Hi' to the more formal 'How do you do?' A written greeting may range from (Gilbert, 1957):

Henrik Ibsen
March 1901   8 Royal Terrace, Fair field
                                        Dublin

Honoured Sir:

to

Constantine P. Curran
N.D. (?) 1904   The Rain, Friday (*sic*)

Dear Curran

to

Helen Joyce
28 August 1935   7 rue Edmond Valentin, Paris 7

Allegretto

Dear complimentary but most suspicious
daughter-in-law

The return and non-return of thanks offers revealing insight into how personal and functional tenors interact. Normally in any kind of social interaction when services are rendered, thanks will be proffered. This rule is defined socially and culturally: it is 'good manners'. The expression of thanks is the linguistic recognition that the action has been performed. The action may be overt—a favour performed, money lent, etc., or simply a kind thought as when we thank someone for having blessed us after a sneeze. Variations in the expression will depend upon the personal tenor. 'Thank you kindly' is fairly formal, 'Thanks' is less so; in geographical dialects 'Ta' is definitely British as is 'Oh, I say, thanks awfully' (the differences in these two may be a reflection of social dialect too). And British visitors to North America are sometimes surprised by the verbal recognition of thanks: 'You're welcome.' Mode can enter into the picture: 'Miss June Smith wishes to express her sincerest gratitude to all those who sent flowers during her recent bereavement' is definitely written text.

Some situations are defined by the absence of recognition of thanks. Use of written mode determines one kind of situation in which thanks may not be recognized. After a weekend in the country one writes to say thanks and the procedure usually ends there. On the telephone one is obliged to murmur 'Not at all. Glad you could come'. Purchasing interactions have their particularities too. The customer usually thanks the shop assistant for all help in selecting, wrapping and paying for the item while the latter thanks the customer for having made the purchase.

Just as some texts are field-dominated, the selections in tenor and mode being largely determined by those of field, some texts are dominated by selections in tenor. The phonological, graphological, syntactic and semantic options of advertising language are all dominated by the functional tenor of persuasion. The use of the superlative, the repetition of particular epithets, and the typical graphological 'tricks' to balance the visual aspect of the message are all marks of the language of publicity.

Typical, too, of functional tenor-dominated language are military and political propaganda (see Chapter three). Solzhenitsyn, in *The Gulag Archipelago* (1973, p. 284), provides some examples of how language is used to hide and distort reality and to intimidate. Particularly effective for these purposes is the use of code words and abbreviations. They sound authoritative and efficient and they easily hide meaning. To understand one must know what the letters stand for (and even then the referential meaning may not be apparent) (e.g. *ibid.*):

ASA   —Anti-Soviet-Agitation
KRD   —Counter-Revolutionary Activity
KRTD—Counter-Revolutionary Trotskyite Activity (and that 'T' made the life of a zek in camp much harder)

PSH   —Suspicion of Espionage (Espionage that went beyond the bounds of suspicion was handed over to a tribunal)

SVPSH—Contacts leading (!) to suspicion of Espionage

KRM   —Counter-Revolutionary Thought

VAS   —Dissemination of Anti-Soviet Sentiments

SOE   —Socially Dangerous Element

SVE   —Socially Harmful Element

PD   —Criminal Activity (a favourite accusation against former camp inmates if there was nothing else to be used against them)

And then, finally, there was the very expansive category:

CHS   —Member of a Family (of a person convicted under one of the foregoing 'letter' categories).

Tenors may have an inclusive–exclusive social function They mark the boundaries of relationships, of group formations. The use of certain markers of tenor, e.g. the code words the underworld uses to refer to itself and to identify police, potential victims and outsiders in general, mark the users as belonging to the group. One of the principal functions of slang is to mark and reinforce identity. The closer one is to the group leaders the more likely one is to use all or most of the indexical markers of the group's dialect. Peripheral members, torn between the group culture and the outside, will exhibit only some of the features (Labov, 1973). Because the intensity of communication among members is greater than between members and non-members, the 'lingo' which develops among them becomes an important identifying mark and a cohesive device. This restricted language, then, develops not as a result of field but as a result of tenor.

Personal relationships can most easily be established and maintained in one-to-one, face-to-face encounters. The development of instantaneous communication methods has made it possible to extend this intimate, direct and immediate form of communication to large numbers of people. However, this great advantage of television can also be its chief weakness.

Television permits the visual and aural transmission of a single message to reach a mass audience. As far as the medium is concerned that mass audience is an undifferentiated one. The consumer is treated largely in that role, as consumer, and not as a member of a particular class, religion, age group, sex, etc. Language, however, offers the possibility of distinguishing addresses along just these lines.

Of course the problem is not created by mass communication. All of us may face difficulties when we are not aware of the social relationships existing between ourselves and the addressee(s). This is especially so in an age of changing values. Our language evolves all the time but we may feel comfortable with new forms of speech only when new values become firmly established. During transition periods we have no rules to guide us. In writing this book, for example, the authors had to decide whether to use 'he' as the unmarked form of gender or to use forms like 'he/she was', 'he/she were', 'person', 'they', etc. Before the women's liberation movement 'he' was accepted as the unmarked form and was understood to refer to all sexes. Now for a certain segment of the English-speaking population 'he' means masculine gender, 'she' means feminine gender and there is, as yet, no unmarked form. Confusion as to acceptability is great and slip-ups like the following job application form can be revealing. A choice was to be made between:

Mr
Mrs
Miss
Ms

as the preferred title. However, a further question asked:

Employer's name: . . .
His title: . . .

The ideologically stalwart might claim that consciousness has not been raised, that women remain the downtrodden mass, as 'proved' by such language. The slip of the writer might, however, only indicate uncertainty as to which grammatical form is correct.

In a similar fashion we learn to avoid the language of racial (religious or ethnic) prejudice, as we become more aware of how language can insult, dehumanize and vilify. Language is traditionally the focus of much anti-discrimination activity (it is the *raison d'être* of anti-defamation leagues). But changing language alone will not in itself change social conditions. Rather the social and political climate must be altered before significant linguistic change can be expected to occur. Language reflects the environment in which it is used, and changing words may only camouflage a situation and new words will develop to describe it—'A rose by any other name will smell as sweet.' So the burden of activity remains in the real world in which language is only one component, albeit a centrally important one.

Chapter six

Register

> We learn above all by taking part in the actual situations
> in which English is used, by attending, and attending
> to ... 'that excellent school, the world'.
> Jeremy Warburg, 'Notions of Correctness'

The concurrence of instances of the contextual categories previously examined (see Chapters three, four and five) produces text varieties called registers. These varieties represent instances of language defined in terms of the similar points they occupy on the continuums of field, mode and personal and functional tenors of discourse. Situationally, these texts reflect similar purposive roles, medium relationships and functional and personal addressee relationships. Language texts which can be placed on the same points within the contextual categories belong to the same register. Register is therefore a useful abstraction linking variations of language to variations of social context.

Register is an instance of language-in-action. It can therefore be described in terms of phonological, lexical and grammatical indexical markers (peculiar to a text) and common-core features (shared by texts). Register is as well the realization of the semantic possibilities of language. It defines what can be *meant* in situation. Register is, then, culturally determined since it is the culture of a society which determines the patterns of environments in which language can occur.

These environments, generalized as situation-types and which include the relevant objects and participants in the event, etc., determine, and in turn are determined by, language use. When we talk about the language of horse-racing, the language of politics, women's language, etc., we imply that there are certain recurrent mutual relationships between features of situation and language use. These relationships make the language of horse-racing different from the language of car-racing, the language of political debate or the language of love. This fact could be trivial in itself—one can readily determine how the language of horse-racing differs from the language of political debate, and how these differences are created by differences in the social context—but register, as the configuration of several contextual features, can draw attention to what changes in situation and context alter what features of language and the reciprocity of this relationship.

Let us illustrate by comparing the language of the text, reproduced in the Appendix, with that of an imagined but not unrealistic situation of another type. Let us imagine, for example, an elegant, expensive French restaurant. The qualifier 'French' refers of course neither to the location nor the nationality of the restaurant but to a particular kind of cuisine. The 'French restaurant' can be considered as an institution having certain characteristics and which can be described in terms of those characteristics. Certainly one could begin to make some predictions about language use from even such a limited situational description. One would expect to find instances of written language (the menu) listing particular kinds of food and probably written in French, in manuscript and not typescript. The customer asks for 'bœuf bourguignon' and not 'beef stew', from a man (the customer is far less likely to be served by a woman in this type of restaurant) addressed as 'Waiter'. The customer is in turn addressed as 'Sir' or 'Madam', or in exceptional circumstances, i.e. if he or she is a frequent customer, by their title plus name—'Mr Jones', 'Miss Smith'.

The location of our text is also a restaurant but of a very different nature. This particular institution is called, in Canadian English, a 'café', or a 'pub' (one word from French, one from English) and is distinguished in this instance from other restaurants of that kind by its location on a university campus. Differences in structure and operation are reflected in the type of language used. The names of foods and drinks available, the manner in which requests are placed by the clientèle reflect the fact that the restaurant is 'quick-service' and has limited capacities for the preparation and consumption of food. The employee may be male or female but is neither a waiter nor a waitress. The customer may be a fellow student, so that the relationship between customer and employee is egalitarian.

There are instances of French-language use in our text but these reflect not the field ('cuisine' of a sort) but the linguistic status of the addresser/addressee. The college recognizes the use of both English and French. This fact is reflected in the switching from one language to the other by bilingual community members.

More predictions can be made about the language used in these two settings if the functional and personal addressee relationships are known. The waiter/customer relationship is reflected in very formal types of address and by certain forms of sentence structure, e.g. the interrogative 'Would you care for something from the bar?' and the contextual request 'May I have the Coquilles Saint Jacques?' The language between customers will be quite different and will vary depending upon the nature of the personal relationships (acquaintances, relatives, lovers) and the purpose of the meeting (*tête-à-tête*, business luncheon, wedding reception).

The functional addressee relationship of the student customer to student employee is somewhat similar to that of the customer/waiter, i.e. a person is using language to obtain from another individual a desired object for which he will exchange money. The interaction is therefore instrumental in kind. The personal relationship is much less formal, however, even between strangers, so that 'What do you want?' or 'Yes?' is perfectly acceptable in this social context.

There are medium differences in the two contexts. The college café has no written menu: customers must verbally request what they want and what there is to have. Employees must recite 'the menu' and succeed more or less depending upon their own individual experience and memory; e.g.:

C: do you have coke↗
E: (nods negatively)

The customer must be prepared to participate in the preparation of the food:

> E: Do you want mustard or mayonnaise↗
> C: mustard↘
> E: on both of them↗ (referring to two sandwiches)
> C: uhh yes

These examples show not only how situation and language are mutually inter-dependent but also how the contextual features interact with each other. Although it is convenient to separate field, mode and tenor it must be remembered that the selection of options in one category may influence the selection of options in another. Contextual features do not merely coincide, they determine one another. Again, to exemplify from the Appendix, the following is a passage where C, a student customer (personal tenor), is making a vocal complaint (mode and functional tenor) about some food (field). E, S and D are student employees.

> C: excuse me I hate to do this but I'm bringing it back
>   'cause it's stale↘
> S: ow well I'll make you another one↘
> C: ok thanks a lot↘ I kinda feel bad doing that but
> D: I guess so eh↗ (laughter) well it's your fault
> C: I do↘
> S: Is that more to your liking↗
> C: yeah ok well I feel rotten bringing it back↗
> overlap {D: well no
>   {S: well if you're not satisfied you should why
> overlap (should you eat something
>   (C: I know . . . I know
>   (S: that you've paid for an' you don't want it
>   ('cause it's not fresh↘

Given the field (the purchase and consumption of food and drink in a restaurant) a vocal complaint is more likely than a written one (although the latter is by no means impossible) since the customer wants an immediate response. The conversational mode in turn influences the functional tenor. The 'tone' of the complaint is 'apologetic' not 'outraged'. It would be unusual to write a letter of complaint with: 'Excuse me. I hate to do this but I'm bringing it back 'cause it's stale.' Face-to-face contact permits a more informal relationship as well, particularly in the egalitarian environment of a North American university.

Mode and field are also inter-related. The offending item is referred to as 'stale', so that we know from the text that it is some kind of food and not a garden hose. However, the item is never mentioned by name. This would only be possible in a situation where the addresser can assume that the addressee knows what the item is, in other words that the addressee is and has been present in the situation. In a letter of complaint one would need to identify the offending article, its defects or one's complaints about it and then request reparation or reimbursement. In an oral situation there is no need to discuss the item. Written mode then makes the social activity 'more' linguistic than the spoken mode.

Register can thus be identified by its relationship to situation. The more typical or stereotyped the situation the more restricted will be the range of options from which choices in field, mode and tenor can be made. Consider, for example, the protocol of diplomatic and royal circles (which extends beyond verbal systems of communication like 'greeting' and address systems to seating arrangements, order of presentation, order of address, etc.). Tenor will be determined by the status that one acquires at birth or marriage, as will be one's rank within the hierarchy (unless as a diplomat one's status is determined by the relative power of one's country). This register is tenor-dominated.

Not all registers, however, are so clearly marked. The range of possible options in unmarked registers is greater, that is to say that there is no fixed or constantly recurring configuration of field, mode and tenor. The configurations which do occur are more variable. For this reason the unmarked registers are much less predictable and are defined with greater difficulty. To illustrate let us examine 'the language of journalism', a variety of language whose name suggests that it must be readily identifiable and distinct from other varieties.

The first distinction one could draw would be that of mode, between the language of 'newscasting' and that of printed reporting. Differences in usage might be found between types of printed works—daily, weekly, bi-monthly newspapers, news magazines, etc.—as well as between individual organs, for example the stylistic differences between the London *Times* and the *Toronto Daily Star*. Similarly, there will be differences noticed between the language on local radio programmes or on disc-jockey shows and that on more serious national-network programmes.

Even within the pages of a single newspaper one can find notable differences in the language of the different 'sections' which can almost be classified at first glance by their style. For example, the following is taken from the front page of a newspaper (*Globe and Mail* (Toronto), 12 July 1975):

Determined To Beat Inflation
Britain limits wages, prices
by Ross Henderson
Globe and Mail Correspondent
London
Prime Minister Harold Wilson yesterday pledged his
'utter determination to beat inflation' with a tough
wage-price policy unveiled in a white paper in the
Commons.

The field, as indicated by vocabulary, suggests 'international economics' or perhaps simply 'international politics'. The items 'tough', 'unveiled', 'white paper', 'Commons', mark this text as one kind of news-reporting just as 'utter determination' marks the citation as a political speech. Compare the text with the following from the same newspaper:

Mr. Wilson's Gamble
It is a most intriguing apparatus which Prime Minister
Harold Wilson proposes to construct to stem Britain's
25 per cent inflation rate. Initially, at least, he sets down
wage and dividend ceilings, but leaves industry to enforce
them. And he does not at this stage provide legal penalties
for companies which decline to act as enforcers.

While the field is the same, there has been a decided shift in functional tenor in the two texts. The first is meant to be an objective news report, a simple narration of events. The second text is editorial commentary designed to explain and possibly to teach. The language used is therefore more evaluative, e.g. 'gamble', 'intriguing', 'enforce', 'enforcers'. The statements are qualified by reservations like 'at least', 'at this stage', which also indicate that the text is presenting an interpretation of fact and not a simple recounting.

For an even more dramatic change compare the above to the following extracts from the 'sports' section where there is a shift in field and in personal tenor:

> Mealia's Late Charge Fails
> Late drama unfolds as Cowan wins Amateur
> by Lawrence Martin
> Globe and Mail Reporter
> Kitchener—For a tense few minutes yesterday, as the Ontario Amateur golf championship drew to a surprisingly suspenseful close, it appeared that heavily favored Gary Cowan might lose.
>
> Mike Mealia, the Toronto Bayview 20-year-old whose phenomenal putting touch had haunted Cowan all week, continued to dazzle on the green, and yesterday, instead of putting for pars, he was sinking them for birdies.

Words like 'putting', 'green', 'pars', 'sinking . . . for birdies', establishes the field as that of golf. Items like 'charge', 'heavily favored', also establish the field as that of sports. The interesting feature of this text is the blatantly evaluative statements of the 'report', e.g. 'tense', 'surprisingly suspenseful', 'phenomenal putting', 'haunted', 'dazzle', etc. The reader/writer relationship is more informal. This informality is increased in the writing of sports-feature writers. For example:

> Here it is July 12 and nobody, anywhere, has awarded the Toronto Argonauts the Grey Cup in July. The old fires are indeed burning low. Argos annually win the Grey Cup in July, in August and September, even in

October, but it is at most 23 years since they won it in November.

The last time they won Lord Grey's old birdbath in November, in fact was 1952—Nov. 29, 1952. Toronto 21, Edmonton 11. That represents a long time between champagne cocktails, whether in one lump or instalments.

Doing such comparative studies will show that the term 'the language of journalism' is rather imprecise. While there may be a need for a term to distinguish the language of the media from other varieties (say, customer/waiter language) it must be kept in mind that individual texts may vary greatly from one another. The unmarked register of journalism offers, then, fewer constraints as regards variations of field, mode and tenor, and is associated with clearly marked situation types. For example:

Stitch armhole facing back to armhole facing front at shoulders and sides.
Pin facing to armhole edge, RIGHT SIDES TOGETHER, matching notches and seams. Stitch.
GRADE seam allowances. Clip curves.
Turn facing to INSIDE. Press.
Top stitch 3/8″ (1 cm) from armhole edge.

This text is obviously an instance of written (mode) instructions (personal and functional tenors) for sewing (field). The language is so restricted that similar instances of language could be found in almost any pattern. Perhaps even more restricted is the following text:

Using No. 10 needles cast on 102 (110: 118: 126) sts.
1st row K2, *P2, K2, rep from * to end.
2nd row P2, *K2, P2, rep from * to end.
Rep 1st and 2nd rows until work measures 4 in.

In this text mode and tenors remain the same but there is a change in field. This text is, of course, part of a set of knitting instructions.

Another aspect of language-in-action deserves further mention. Halliday (1975b) has pointed out in connection with field that the social activity of the linguistic event can change although the field remains the same. The activity can be placed on a 'more' or 'less' linguistic cline. In other words, the focus of the activity may be language or it may be some particular action. The focus of activity in the preparation of a meal is the cooking itself. Whatever language occurs may be quite limited in relation to the cooking, e.g. requests for particular materials, for assistance, etc. The major part of the dialogue between participants may be more concerned with topics of personal interest, i.e. health, the weather, recent activities and other associated topics related to phatic communion. The focus of activity of a cooking lesson, however, is language itself. Language is being used to teach about the preparation of food. This event would be more 'linguistic' than the first event.

Placing behavioural events on a 'more' or 'less' linguistic cline helps to explain why so much of conversation is unintelligible. In many instances in the text of the Appendix the dialogue between the client/employee is quite limited. It can be reduced to an initiating remark—the request (greeting is optional since facial expression can be substituted for verbalization), the statement of price (also optional since many customers know what it is) and a terminating remark ('Thanks' usually: this, too, is optional). In other words an entire transaction could be carried out and the only absolutely necessary speech might be the remark 'Tea please'. The activity itself is largely non-linguistic. Complaining about a stale sandwich is, on the other hand, 'more' linguistic.

The repeated association of field, mode and tenors of discourse in situation-type creates expectancies. This is suggested by the notion of predictability of register. Expectations may or may not be met, however. The marked register of greeting and address promotes smooth social interaction when participants know and abide by the rules. When they do not, friction can be caused among the participants, a social 'gaffe' perhaps committed. The ultimate use of this type of association may be the 'soft-sell' advertising technique which depends for its persuasive effect on the constant repetition of words like 'new', 'improved', 'brighter', 'whiter', which have positive connotations, and the product name.

At the same time, great literature may often make its impact by constantly not meeting the linguistic expectations of the addressee. Writers will consciously alter normal patterns of form and substance, will 'play' with the semantic possibilities offered by language in order to create an innovative work that draws our attention afresh to human experience and its verbalization. The study of literary style may be viewed from this perspective, in terms of predictability of patterns, of shifts and changes from linguistic norms (Spencer and Gregory, 1964; Halliday, 1973).

Register as text variety is 'embedded' in situation. It reflects individual experience and therefore the individual capacity 'to mean'. Register reflects both the on-going activity of the situation in which the text belongs but also the previous experiences of the individual. Who has not felt the embarrassment of being in a new situation and not knowing 'what to say' or perhaps just as importantly 'how to say it'? Control of several registers and the ability to shift from one to another is implied in good social behaviour. But control of a range of different registers results from experiencing different kinds of situations demanding different kinds of behaviour. So register range will be revealed in idiolect. Social patterns will also be revealed by the individual's capacity to shift registers in so far as an individual's experience is to some degree a function of vertical and horizontal social stratification.

Register-shifting may indicate formal education and a conscious awareness of linguistic norms. However, education must not be viewed as the only determinant of this kind of linguistic skill. The cocktail-party bore who can only 'talk shop' is an all-too-common educated phenomenon. Moreover, register-shifting may involve questions of the range of meanings available to and used by sub-cultural groups. Individually, limited ranges of meaning could in fact result from the systematic restriction of meaning at the level of social groups as determined by patterns of social interaction inherent in social structure. We return, therefore, to the mutual relationship of language and culture.

It is perhaps easy to understand how field is determined by the ways in which a society organizes, analyses and names its experience and orders it in systems of knowledge; or that mode will be strictly determined by the availability of specific symbolic mediums, and so by the technology of that society; or that roles and relationships inherent in tenors of discourse depend upon the institutional and individual roles that make up the social structure. The situation-types, the environments in which language can occur, will be determined by culture. The 'context of situation' can be placed within the 'context of culture' (Malinowski, 1923; Firth, 1935, 1937, 1950; Halliday, 1974, 1975b).

It is not so readily seen how the social structure can determine the range of individual meaning potential, the capacity 'to mean' in situation, or how, within the complete range of possibilities inherent in a given culture, only certain 'areas' are selected and used in a systematic way by particular cultural sub-groups. These patterns of meaning potential, the linguistic codes which constitute strategies of language use and which link language and social structure, will be discussed in Chapter seven.

Code

> Concepts of 'time' and 'matter' are not given in
> substantially the same form by experience to all men but
> depend upon the nature of the language or languages
> through the use of which they have been developed. They
> do not depend so much upon ANY ONE SYSTEM
> (e.g., tense, or nouns) within the grammar as upon the
> ways of analyzing and reporting experience which have
> become fixed in the language as integrated 'fashions of
> speaking' and which cut across the typical grammatical
> classifications, so that such a 'fashion' may include lexical,
> morphological, syntactic and otherwise systematically
> diverse means coordinated in a certain frame of
> consistency.
> Benjamin Lee Whorf, *Language, Thought and Reality:
> Selected Writings of Benjamin Lee Whorf*

We have emphasized in Chapter one the importance of looking
at language as a social phenomenon, as a type of meaningful
interaction among individuals in a social context. Language is
therefore considered to be more than lexical, grammatical or
phonological systems and structures. We can regard it as
behaviour relating the participants in a speech event to their
environment, to each other and to the medium of communication itself. Text as an operational instance of language
implies, therefore, a common social and cultural 'meaning'
system in addition to a shared system of verbal symbols. This
is not simply another way of saying that words have meanings
and are composed of sounds—'phonemes', or letters—
'graphemes'. Words change their meanings according to
context. Word-meaning is neither fixed nor stable. Word-
meaning can be considered to be meaning-in-use, the 'living'
word as it appears in situation. Meaning realized in recurrent

and typical situations can itself be seen as part of a larger system of meaning to which members of the community have access. This system of potential meaning is the culture itself. When we say that language is choice we suggest that language-in-use implies the selection of all possible meanings inherent in this extensive meaning system called culture. Only certain ranges of meaning will be relevant to a given situation and these meanings will be encoded in grammatical and lexical options.

Examination of individual utterances reveals extensive variation, even in utterances produced by the same speaker. Language seems to be characterized by such variability, yet participants in a speech event have little difficulty in decoding messages in spite of changes in the environment or in the content of the message. It would appear that not every change is pertinent to the interpretation of the speech event. The 'infinite variability' of language does not pose insurmountable difficulties to communication because we find similarities between utterances, and between speech events, which enable us to decode the message. As Halliday (1975b) suggests, variables can themselves be meaningful since social values tend to be associated with them: 'sexy' women in television advertisements often have husky voices in imitation of Mae West, comedians and comediennes successfully portray children by giggling, squealing, stuttering, etc. The successful interpretation of the message depends upon the association of given social values with the particular formal or phonic features used.

Whorf suggested as early as 1936 ('A Linguistic Consideration of Thinking in Primitive Communities', in Whorf, 1956) that linguistics is concerned primarily with meaning, meaning being given an enlarged sense. The particular problem posed for sociolinguistics as an independent study is the examination and correlation of linguistic and sociological phenomena. If it is true that language reflects society then it should be possible to determine the specific ways in which this reflection occurs by showing how individual social factors determine the selection of individual linguistic features. Seeking such relationships involves more than identifying social correlates with formal and phonological variation, as we have done so far in discussing dialect.

Hasan (1973) has suggested that the descriptive techniques of dialectology, although offering interesting insights into the ways in which varieties differ from one another, do not explain the sociological basis of differences in language use. Both Hasan (1973) and Halliday (1975a, 1975b) have suggested that variation of language use must be related to something other than the linguistic system. Variation must be linked to an independent theory of social development and change. The concept 'social dialect' is a useful descriptive category to cover differences of formal and linguistic features; however, to describe variability at the cultural level a different kind of abstraction is required.

To do so we must think of culture and the social structural system as a system of meanings. The culture of a society incorporates all possible meaningful behaviour (linguistic and otherwise) possible within that society, the beliefs and attitudes associated with it, including the arts and sciences as we usually think of them. Culture therefore subsumes the social structure, or the organization of roles and potential relationships among members of the society. It subsumes shared values of the society (including the value systems of sub-groups). Culture includes systems of knowledge about the environment, about the past, about objects, things, ideas, etc. The social system is a social semiotic (Halliday, 1975b); a system of symbolic action, of organized meaning potential.

Behaviour, therefore, can be meaningful. Language is only one type of meaningful behaviour. Gesture, facial expression, smoke signals, are other types of non-linguistic, meaningful behaviour (writing systems like Braille or a system like semaphore are all based on language and therefore constitute manifestations of linguistic behaviour). At the cultural level of analysis these systems are all possible options which can be made within the 'context of culture' (Malinowski, 1923) of a given society. The context of culture is in turn actualized in a context of situation. Both an Italian and an American when stuck in traffic have the option of shouting and swearing or of honking their car horns. It may be more usual, however, for Italians to honk their automobile horns than it would be for North Americans. We see in this context of situation a typical, recurrent environment in which language events may take place, depending always on the larger context of culture. Situation-type therefore implies context of culture since the former is only one semiotic structure in the entire range of possible semiotic structures inherent in the culture.

The social system is therefore regarded as a system of behavioural patterns which language interprets and realizes. Meaning is not, contrary to the popular expression, merely a question of semantics; rather, there is meaning to be found at all levels of analysis. To determine how this occurs requires that we examine how language 'means', that is to say the various meaningful functions that language performs. Describing what language does has enabled Halliday (based on earlier work done by the Prague Circle), for example, to develop a model of semantic macro-functions: the ideational (experiential and logical), the inter-personal and the textual. In other words, language has a 'referential' function, it names and describes things in the environment; language has a social function, establishing roles and relationships; language has its own way of doing things and relating to the rest of our behaviour (cf. Chapters three and eight).

These macro-functions belong to the linguistic system. They are linguistic variants of 'can mean'. The ways in which the meaning potentials of the social system are actually organized into semantic categories have yet to be explained. To do this we must step beyond the linguistic system and its levels of phonology, lexis and grammar, and semantics, to try to relate the social system to the linguistic system. In this manner we can determine how the meaning potential present in the social system determines the organization of meaning and therefore influences the selection of formal linguistic items. We need an intermediary concept linking language to culture.

This intermediary concept has been provided, in part at least, by the work of the sociologist Basil Bernstein and his colleagues at the University of London Institute of Education.

Bernstein, interested in language as a part of the socialization process, has investigated the relationship of language to educability and social class in England. He wanted to develop a theory capable of explaining how 'linguistic failure' is linked to 'educational failure' and how failure in the school system reflects the English social structure. The problem of low success rates among working-class children is not unique, of course, to England. The problem has also been studied in the USA but more specifically as it relates to black children in urban ghettos. The English and American studies are not therefore based on identical experiences. They do, however, both concentrate on structural problems. The language of the working-class child was often considered to be deficient; some suggested that these children had no language at all. Others considered their language to be structurally 'just different', the school system favouring the dialect of the middle class. Bernstein has examined the problem from the point of view of use. Different classes, he found, have different ways of using language, different 'strategies' for meaning, different 'fashions' of speaking. Class structure created different linguistic codes.

Bernstein found that language, used in certain key socializing contexts, was a principal factor in the acquisition of the child's social identity. The child learns who he is, in terms of the social structure, through language—that language which surrounds him in his daily activities, that language which is directed to him personally, particularly as it is used to control his behaviour. The child learns how to relate to others, i.e. children learn how to address their elders, strangers, each other, in control situations; for example, 'You mustn't interrupt Aunt Edith when she's talking' or perhaps, 'Don't talk back to your mother.'

An individual can and does possess numerous distinct roles in a lifetime. Even in the course of a single day he will act first in one capacity and then in another. Some of these roles are long term, features of permanent (or reasonably so) relationships. A given individual can be husband or wife, mother or father (depending on the 'reasonably permanent status' of sex roles), lawyer, citizen, etc. These roles may change at some time, hence the 'reasonably' (couples divorce, workers lose or change their occupations and so on). However, while the possibility exists that these long-term roles may change with time, an obvious contrast can be made between them and more immediate roles which reflect the context of situation. A lawyer, normally functioning in his long-term occupational role in court, might be required to assume others in specific instances, e.g. 'accused' or 'witness to an accident'.

The social identity of the individual will result from a configuration of roles he possesses or can possess. Both long-term and situational roles are created by the social system. They reflect the culture—the role of 'prime minister' can only exist in a system possessing a parliamentary form of government; the role of 'potential purchaser of meat in a butcher's shop' depends upon the existence of certain eating habits (one would not expect such a role in a vegetarian society), and on a particular type of economic organization (in a society of farmers who slaughter and butcher their own meat and poultry this role might not be filled). Because the culture determines the role system, it determines the nature of interaction between different members of the system. Culture is therefore reflected in variations of verbal interaction which depend on role relationships. Bernstein has developed the concept of code to show how the social system determines and is reflected in linguistic differences.

Code determines the meaning potential of the individual. It is, as we have suggested, a strategy or plan of linguistic use. The social system determines the entire range of meanings available to the community. Code can be seen to embody a range of meanings access to which is determined by the place the individual occupies in the social structure. Code controls the verbal repertoire of the individual, his capacity to encode meaning lexically and grammatically. Code therefore determines which options will be selected as appropriate to the given situation.

We return again to the idea of language as behaviour. Certain types of behaviour only will be appropriate to a given situation. This is not simply a question of social etiquette.

Communication depends upon participants being able to interpret and anticipate behaviour in situation. Unkind words said with a smile or a wink may not be taken seriously. If they are, we say that a misunderstanding has occurred, communication has broken down. Frequently, though, appropriateness to situation can be seen as a question of etiquette if we regard the latter as simply conventions of personal interaction. Etiquette constitutes rules of social behaviour. Code enters the picture in determining how situation is interpreted, how meaning is organized.

Bernstein postulates two types of code which reflect two different principles of semantic organization. Each code orientates the user to a specific type of meaning which is itself a function of the type of relationship that the user enters into. Code is therefore the product of individual experience. At the same time code directs further experience in that it determines the interpretation of meaning in speech events. The codes, elaborated and restricted, are acquired through exposure to different speech models. They embody two types of meaning. The concept of code has therefore two facets—the semiotic and the linguistic. Both the speech models and the semiotic functions are referred to as universalistic or particularistic.

Universalistic meaning is meaning made verbally explicit. The addresser does not assume that the addressee shares the meaning. It tends therefore to be individuated and personal. The particularistic meaning, on the other hand, is verbally implicit. The addresser does assume that the meaning is shared. It tends therefore to be 'public' meaning.

The universalistic speech model is one available to all members of the speech community. The particularistic speech model, however, has a limited distribution; it is available only to certain groups in the social structure. The restricted code tends to employ a universal speech model coupled with particularistic meaning. This code orientates the user to express linguistically ascribed position, inclusive and binding social relationships. As Bernstein says (1971) it emphasizes the 'We' over the 'I', that is to say it is used to express commonality and public values. The elaborated code tends to employ a universalistic meaning and a particularistic speech model. The elaborated code orientates the user to achieved status; it places the 'I' above the 'We'. It is used to express individuality, to maintain social distance and to express personal values.

The importance of the code theory in education lies in the fact that the school system requires the use of an elaborated code but not all students have access to it. The importance of this theory to sociology lies in the fact that the differential access to the elaborated code does not occur randomly but rather is controlled by the class system. Lower-working-class urban children in England, Bernstein suggests, tend to have only a restricted code. Middle-class children possess both a restricted and an elaborated code. The two groups enter into different types of relationships and learn to express meaning in different ways through language. They do not use language for the same functions, some of which, it seems, are necessary for the school situation. When the lower-working-class child is expected implicitly to exploit language for functions he normally does not express verbally, a discontinuity is created between his home and his school environment. He has learned to verbalize a certain range of meanings in his home and when he enters the school another range of meanings is required. There is, then, a very subtle but none the less very real sense in which what is taught is personally irrelevant for this child. The school system does not talk to him about what he knows. Middle-class children possessing both codes, experience no such discontinuity. They can use language for those functions required by the school.

In order to illustrate we shall use two passages representative of the two codes constructed by Peter Hawkins of the University of London Institute of Education Sociological Research Unit (Bernstein, 1971, p. 178). Hawkins analysed the speech of two groups of five-year-old children. Both working-class and middle-class children were confronted with a series of four pictures: showing some boys playing football; the football breaking the window of a house; a woman looking out of the broken window and a man making a threatening gesture; the children moving away. The informants were asked to describe

the story in the picture. Based on his results Hawkins produced
the following stories:

Middle-class example:
Three boys are playing football and one boy kicks the
ball and it goes through the window the ball breaks the
window and the boys are looking at it and a man comes
out and shouts at them because they've broken the
window so they run away and then that lady looks out
of her window and she tells the boys off.

Working-class example:
They're playing football and he kicks it and it goes
through there and it breaks the window and they're
looking at it and he comes out and shouts at them
because they've broken it so they run away and then
she looks out and she tells them off.

To a person familiar with the test situation the stories may
appear to be fundamentally the same. The differences, however, are both striking and important. The middle-class example
makes the elements of the story—objects, participants, actions,
etc.—verbally explicit. The story is, in fact, independent of the
test situation. One does not need to be in the situation to understand the story. The working-class example, however, is
situation-bound because of the consistent use of pronominal-
ization. However, the capacity spontaneously to render meaning explicit in language is necessary for success in most
contemporary school systems.

It should be apparent from these examples, however, that
code is not synonymous with social dialect. The grammatical
differences in these examples are slight (we cannot, of course,
comment on the possible phonological variations of the
children's stories as if they were spoken). Code refers to principles of semantic organization. These principles are reflected
in lexical and grammatical selections, it is true, but the formal
features used are important indirectly and only as they reflect
semantic differences. In fact the formal features used by both
classes may be the same or similar. Bernstein has stressed that

the restricted code is possessed by both groups. Ostensibly then both groups could say the same thing in similar situations calling for the use of restricted code. Social dialect, however, is a contextual category referring to text and to formal variation. It implies semantic organization but emphasis is on text associated with socio-situational variables. Its use as a descriptive category is that it permits the isolation and description of specific kinds of formal variation. The variations produced by code differences reflect not features of the user but rather features of the user's use of language in situation. Code influences register (see Chapter six) not dialect.

The educational problems of England, as they are posed by Bernstein (and his views are disputed), can therefore be seen to be somewhat different from those of the USA. The work done on Black English by linguists like William Labov and Raven McDavid Jr is dialectal studies dealing with features of American Negro speech: for example, the loss of certain phonological contrasts /θ/ becoming more like /f/, /ð/ becoming more like /v/; simplification of final consonantal clusters, e.g. loss of final /t/ or /d/ in words like 'fast', 'send', etc.; use of the copula 'be', e.g. 'he be' (+adjective). When American writers speak of 'code-switching' they are not referring to code as it has been used here. Code-switching refers to dialect-switching. This is not to say that some of the educational problems of American ghetto children may not be related to code in Bernstein's sense. The studies done on Black English have concentrated on structure and have not dealt with the distribution and use of restricted code (see, for example, Bereiter and Engelmann, 1966). Certain linguists have specifically tried to refute the work of the 'verbal-deprivation' sociologists who suggest that Black English does not permit certain types of conceptualization and abstraction, i.e. that it is more a code in Bernstein's sense. Labov particularly has studied non-standard Negro speech from this perspective (see Labov et al., 1965, 1968; Labov, 1966, 1970, 1972a).

Code determines the verbal repertoire or the range of 'styles' an individual can possess, since it determines the range of meanings which that person can express through linguistic means. It constitutes a 'frame of speaking', a 'strategy of use', and therefore determines how an individual will interpret situation. It also controls the ways in which a user will actualize the meaning potential of the social system in register which results from a configuration of situational features. Code determines the ways in which specific formal features relate (through the contextual features of field, mode and tenor) to situation. The contextual determinants of text have been discussed in preceding chapters (in lexical, grammatical and phonological terms) as kinds of language use and as components of the speech situation (see Chapter one and Chapters three to five). They will be discussed in the final chapter as part of a conceptual framework for representing, in contextual terms this time, the semiotic environment of the text. Let us note here simply that these features, which can be directly related to the linguistic levels, can also be linked to social structure and to the context of culture. A direct connection can be made between the linguistic 'can mean' and the social 'can mean'. The connective concept is code.

Chapter eight

Conclusion: textual varieties, meaning and social context

> The disciplines and techniques of linguistics are directed
> to assist us in making statements of meaning. Indeed the
> main concern of descriptive linguistics is to make
> statements of meaning.
>
> J. R. Firth, *Essays and Studies*

What has been discussed so far throughout this book can be
seen in relation to the recent development by M. A. K.
Halliday of a social theory of language (see, in particular,
Halliday, 1973, 1974, 1975a, 1975b and forthcoming). The
approach he takes is functional: it means (Halliday, 1973,
p. 7)

> first of all, investigating how language is used: trying to
> find out what are the purposes that language serves for
> us, and how we are able to achieve these purposes
> through speaking and listening, reading and writing. But
> it also means more than this. It means seeking to explain
> the nature of language in functional terms: seeing
> whether language itself has been shaped by use, and if
> so, in what ways—how the form of language has been
> determined by the functions it has evolved to serve.

A functional approach necessitates viewing language from
a social perspective and seeing it as a form of behaviour
potential—what the user can do; behaviour which involves
language is the result of linguistic or meaning potential—what
the user can mean; this meaning potential is realized in the
language system as lexico-grammatical potential—what the
user can say. The adult speaker operates constantly and simul-
taneously within language's ideational (language as 'content'),
inter-personal (language as 'inter-action') and textual (language
as 'texture') functions. A grammar can then be seen as 'the

linguistic device for hooking up the selections in meaning which are derived from the various functions of language and realizing them in a unified structural form' (Halliday, *op. cit.*, p. 42).

This kind of approach to the description of language has to be wary of the tradition in linguistics of taking the sentence (however defined or described) as the key, or top, unit of description. People do not speak, in the sense of 'behave linguistically', in sentences. Sentence is a grammatical unit and a construct of the grammarian. Language users are choosing a form of doing that involves linguistic meaning, they are 'meaning' linguistically. The key unit, then, in a functional, socially orientated description, has to be a unit of meaning, in other words, a semantic unit. Halliday and Hasan (1976) have suggested the unit 'text'. Text, in this sense, is not just a kind of super-sentence, something that is longer than a sentence but of the same kind. (Of course, from one point of view we can use the term 'text' for a string of sentences or a sentence that realizes a text, but we can also be aware that such a string, or such a sentence, is the lexico-grammatical realization of the text rather than the text itself.) Text, in the Halliday–Hasan sense, is a meaning concept, a semantic unit. As physical events, texts themselves are 'instances of linguistic interaction in which people actually engage' (Halliday, 1975b, p. 24). Viewed more abstractly a text is 'what is meant' and is the consequence of a set of choices from the total set of options that a language makes possible, the range of semantic choices members of a culture have access to in their language. Halliday (*op. cit.*, p. 25) points out that interpreted in terms of Malinowski's concept of the context of culture (Malinowski, 1923, 1935; Firth, 1957; Palmer (ed.), 1968), this means the entire semantic system of the language, which is 'a fiction, something we cannot hope to describe; interpreted in the context of situation, it is the particular semantic system or set of sub-systems, which is associated with a particular type of situation or social context', and 'this too is a fiction; but it is something that may be more easily describable'.

Halliday's suggestion is that a particular situation-type can be interpreted as a semiotic structure that can be represented as a complex of three dimensions: the on-going social activity (field), the role relationships involved (tenors), and the symbolic or rhetorical channel (mode). He maintains that field, mode and tenor can, from this point of view, now be considered as more than just 'kinds of language use', or simple 'components of the speech setting'. He sees them rather as 'a conceptual framework for representing the social context as the semiotic environment in which people exchange meanings', and register can then be seen as 'the configuration of semantic resources that the member of a culture typically associates with a situation type'; he points out that 'both the situation and the register associated with it can be described to varying degrees of specificity' and that 'the existence of registers is a fact of everyday experience—speakers have no difficulty in recognizing the semantic options and combinations of options that are "at risk" under particular environmental conditions' (*op. cit.*, p. 26).

Halliday's recent work is the latest in the development of the concept of situation in linguistics, which goes back as far as Wegener (1885). In the ethnography of language Malinowski proposed and developed his 'context of situation' (1923, 1935), and a 'close-to-the-ground' notion of situation played a key part in Sir Alan Gardiner's *The Theory of Speech and Language* (1932). J. R. Firth (1950, 1957; and in Palmer (ed.), 1968) made the concept somewhat more abstract, pointing out that the linguist was to be less concerned with the particular details of the setting of a particular speech event and more with context of situation as an abstract description of the environment by way of textually relevant general categories. He was aware that the relevant context of situation of some texts (e.g. from literature) was something quite other than what is actually taking place about the act of speaking or writing, listening or reading. Gregory (1967) recognized the need both for abstraction and constant renewal with the details of actual texts, and distinguished situation from context. Situation was used for 'the study of those extra-textual features, linguistic and non-linguistic, which have high potential relevance to statements of meaning about the texts of language events'; context was reserved for 'the correlations of formally described linguistic features, groupings of such features within texts and abstracted from them, with those situational features themselves constantly recurrent and relevant to the understanding of language events.' This meant that situation was seen not as a level of language or linguistics but as an aspect of the description of language events. Context was seen as a level of language because its concern is with certain patterns and correlations of patterns which enable us to identify certain behaviour as linguistic behaviour.

Halliday's subsequent further increase of abstraction and organization of related sets of options—behavioural, semantic and lexico-grammatical—within the three macro-functions, ideational, inter-personal and textual, provides, potentially, a genuine basis for what Pike (1967) attempted: an approach to language in relation to a unified theory of the structure of human behaviour. At the same time, however, as register is seen as 'the selection of meanings that constitute the variety to which a text belongs' it can also be seen 'as a particular selection of words and structures' (Halliday, 1975b, p. 26), as is a text.

A text, we have said, is a piece of language that forms a unified whole, and is not just a collection of unrelated sentences; it has 'texture' and it derives this texture from the fact that it functions as a unity with respect to its environment. It can be seen to hang together internally by way of cohesion (Halliday and Hasan, *op. cit.*). Cohesion is present when the interpretation of an element in the text presupposes something other than itself and that something is also explicitly realized in the text. Then the two elements, the presupposing and the presupposed, form part of the same text, and constitute a cohesive 'tie'. In English, reference, ellipsis, substitution, conjunction and lexical cohesion are the sources of text formation beyond sentence boundaries: the structures of units from the sentence down, i.e. clause, group and word, are of course, themselves text-forming.

The relationship of presupposing/presupposed can be seen in the following simple examples of each kind of tie.

Reference:
   John's arrived. *He*'s in the kitchen.
Substitution:
   I've lost my *lighter*. I'll have to find a new *one*.
Ellipsis:
   Are you *going to the dance*?
   I *can't*.
Conjunction:
   He failed his exams. Consequently *he's back for another
   year*.
Lexical cohesion:
   He got to the *shop* just in time. Then he couldn't reach
   the *counter*.

Ties of these kinds are, then, what internally makes a text
hang together. But in judging, consciously or unconsciously,
the status of a piece of language as to whether or not it is text
or just a random collection of sentences, the reader or hearer
not only responds to linguistic clues (internal evidence) but
also to situational clues (external evidence). In responding to
a text we generally take into account all we know of the environment: what is going on, who is involved, as well as what part
language is playing; and, as has been noted, register is the concept that deals with these relations. So Halliday and Hasan
(*op. cit.*, p. 23) assert that:

in general, if a passage hangs together as a text it will
display a consistency of register. In other words the
texture involves more than the presence of semantic
relations of the kind we refer to as cohesive, the
dependence of one element on another for its
interpretation. It involves also some degree of coherence
in the actual meanings expressed: not only or even mainly
in the content, but in the total selection from the
semantic resources of the language, including the various
socio-personal or expressive components—the moods,
modalities, intensities, and other forms of the intrusion
of the speaker into the speech situation.

And so a text, the most crucial unit of language, is a passage of discourse which is both consistent in register, and so 'coherent with respect to the context of the situation', and which is coherent with respect to itself in so far as it displays cohesion. Neither condition is sufficient without the other. Of course in real life, as Halliday and Hasan (*op. cit.*, p. 24) point out, the nearest we get to non-text, 'leaving aside the works of those poets and prose writers [and some comedians] who deliberately set out to create non-text, is probably in the speech of young children and in bad translations.' What is more important than text/non-text decisions in a consideration of language variety and social contexts is the *more* or *less* of texture, and how much of the interpretive weight is internal and how much external, and how different situation-types are related to differently formed texts: formal written texts sound funny when they are spoken, and conversations look odd when written down; children's essays often make sense situationally although the teacher knows there is something wrong about how they are 'hung together' as a piece of language. The recognition and the description of the internal and external conditions for text have high potential for use in linguistic pedagogy and applied stylistics.

The major concern of this book has, however, been with language varieties as 'kinds of language use', 'particular selections of words and structures', associated with 'components of the speech setting' and so in conclusion we will discuss eight major uses of the distinction and description of varieties.

Their use in the language teacher's choice of materials

Many of the materials used in teaching English to speakers of other languages (and in teaching French in grammar and high schools in the English-speaking world) have not always been appropriately chosen and have frequently been restricted to too narrow a band of the spectrum of sub-languages that constitute the target language (cf. Halliday, McIntosh and Strevens, 1964). There are also some second-language teaching situations in which the learner has a primary need for a thorough grasp of a 'restricted' language within the target language, as do research students needing to have a reading access to materials within their field of discourse in the other language. Mention in this regard could be made of the work J. R. Firth instigated in teaching Allied pilots enough 'ground to air' and 'place to place' Japanese to be able to intercept and understand Japanese pilots and their ground control during the Second World War.

First-language learning in bilingual situations has its own problems. In the French of Franco-Ontarian students we have noticed both a restricted range of personal tenors and an inconsistent use of such tenors in several registers. In their written work there are switches from informal to very formal usages, sometimes within the same sentence. So one gets 'familiar' or informal uses like

courir+*après*+complement
partir+*à*+infinitive

alongside expressions such as

à cause que (rather than *parce que*)

and

tous deux (rather than *tous les deux*).

In Standard European French both these expressions are considered a little archaic and hence very formal. They are quite common in what might be called Standard Canadian French. However, the francophone community generally insists on a variety unmarked as to geographical dialect for the written mode. Again, many Franco-Ontarian students learn to adapt to the phonology of English quite well but tend to be restricted, grammatically and lexically, to informal personal tenors which they use in situations requiring more formal tenors. The social effects can often be devastating, particularly if the speaker has a near native-like pronunciation. He or she gives the impression to other English speakers of being rude, indifferent, perhaps not very intelligent, just because of the use of the 'wrong' tenor. On the other hand, some quite proficient

Nigerian speakers of English have difficulty hitting the right note in informal tenors, perhaps because they tend to use their native language in more familiar or intimate situations. Their informal English tenors often sound out-of-date, as though they have been learnt from the novel literature of a few decades ago. When faced with such problems both teacher and learner can benefit from an explicit consciousness and growing knowledge of the variety dimensions of language.

Native speakers of a language such as English, particularly if they come from a restricted code (see Chapter seven) or non-standard (see Chapter two) background, need to have their awareness of what is the multiplicity of the language systematically extended so that they increase their range of register control. Indeed this is necessary for all students and scholars of English at all levels. Many university departments of English on both sides of the Atlantic ought to realize that they have a responsibility to inform their students not only about the literary language but about the rest of the language which throughout time has allowed the literary artist to 'create' experience by manipulating the common verbalizations of common experiences. If we are actively aware that the fundamental characteristic of a language is that it is the noises we make with our faces and the scribbles we make with our hands in order to live, we cannot but be sensible that it is this which makes literature possible. Nobody now writes novels in Latin, except perhaps to win prizes for writing novels in Latin, because so very few now make Latin noises in order to live. The language of literature is only partially known and appreciated if it is not seen and known in relation to the creative multiplicity of the non-literary users of language that surround it and feed it (cf. Spencer and Gregory, 1964; Benson and Greaves, 1973; Gregory, 1974).

In the making of rhetorics

During the last fifty years a great deal of linguistics has been stridently opposed to prescriptivism and it was probably necessary that it should be; there had been and was much rule-giving about language usage based on an imperfect and incomplete idea of what it is. However, there can be nothing but health in prescriptions for how to use language well and effectively if they are based upon sound and thorough descriptions of the appropriate linguistic and situational conditions of the type of text in question. Such a prescription is what is meant here by a 'rhetoric' (cf. Warburg, 1961).

In the judgment of correctness or, preferably, appropriateness of usage

There seems to be a general human compulsion to pass judgment on other people's use of language. When one is aware of the fecund variety of a language, and that so many of the traditional criteria for correctness are based on untenable criteria ('etymology', 'grammatical unchangeability', 'logic', social judgments masquerading as linguistic judgments) then measures of appropriateness can be one's concern rather than absolute standards of good and bad. The appropriateness of items in a text can be judged according to whether or not they occur frequently enough or are sufficiently like other customary usages to be recognized as appropriate in the particular variety demanded by the situation in which they occur. 'This is not to take a permissive view of language, a view that "anything will do", it is to take a productive view, it aims to extend people's awareness and appreciation of the ever-developing range of varying language habits summed up by the word "English" [or, for that matter, 'French', 'German', 'Yoruba', 'Chinese', etc.]' (Gregory, 1969, p. 7; and cf. also Halliday, McIntosh and Strevens, 1964).

In the study of style, especially in the establishment of relevant norms for comparison and contrast

'The style of a discourse is the message carried by the frequency distributions and transitional probabilities of its linguistic features, especially as they differ from those of the same features in the language as a whole'; so wrote Bernard

Bloch (1953, pp. 40–1). However, as Enkvist (1964, p. 25) pointed out, such a definition 'gives us the formidable and theoretically objectionable task of using the entire language as a norm.' It suggests what Abercrombie (1963b) has called a 'pseudo-procedure'. On the other hand a 'placing of the text' as to where it stands as regards the dialectal and diatypic varieties of the language, a locating of it on dimensions of time, place, social class, purposive role, medium relationship, functional and personal addressee relationships, can point to what are relevant norms for comparison and contrast (cf. Enkvist, Spencer and Gregory, 1964, pp. 27–32, 85–90). The heterogeneity of language has been ordered, the wilderness tamed a little. Furthermore, the semantic gain of seeing a text in its dialect, register and situational framework is crucial to the process of what has been termed interpretive stylistics (cf. Gregory, 1974; Handscombe, 1970), a very central kind of literary criticism which aims to answer the question 'What does it mean?' of a literary text by way of the questions 'What is it?' and 'How is it?'

In the establishment of translation equivalence

There has been a growing awareness that translation is not just a matter of item-to-item equivalence, or indeed of group of items to group of items, or structure to structure; rather it is a matter of text-to-text equivalence which involves variety and register considerations (see Catford, 1965; Palmer (ed.), 1968). Source and target language have to be described in terms of text, and not just sentence, to ensure semantic equivalence.

In the collection and assessment of a representative corpus for descriptive statements about a language

It has already been asserted (Chapter four) that until recently many grammars of English, and indeed of French, German, etc., have been based on, and adequately describe, only a por- tion of what is English (or French, or German, etc.), usually the reasonably formal and written or written to be spoken. Even Jespersen's great grammatical works on English (1909–49, 1933) draw most of their citations from literature (Shakespeare and Galsworthy resound through their pages), and Charles Carpenter Fries's famous *Structure of English* (1952), despite its many virtues, suffers from being based on a corpus of telephone conversations. Transformational-generative grammarians have tended to dismiss the need for a corpus and have relied on their informed intuitions, which may be one reason why their grammars have to reject so much of the language people really use as being 'ill-formed'. A corpus which is hospitable to the many fields, modes and tenors of a language and its major social and geographical dialects (if relevant) would seem to be one best suited to ensure that the 'exceptions' to grammatical 'rules' become rarer and that descriptions become more comprehensively reflective of what a language really is. *A Grammar of Contemporary English* (Quirk, Greenbaum, Leech and Svartik, 1972), based as it is on the Survey of Educated English Usage conducted from University College London, has the strength of being more sensitive to the varieties and social contexts of the language being described than any other grammar the present authors have encountered.

In making more sophisticated the institutional labelling of items in dictionaries

The great unabridged dictionaries of the English language— *The Oxford English Dictionary*, *Webster's Third International Dictionary of the English Language*, and the more recent *Random House Dictionary of the English Language* and *American Heritage Dictionary of the English Language*—all recognize the value of giving an indication of what variety of the language an item, or an item as limited by one of their definitions, might be found in. So they use abbreviated labels such as *obs.* for 'obsolete', *arch.* for 'archaic' (both reflecting temporal dialect), *Brit.* and *Am.* for 'British' and 'American' (reflecting geographical dialect), *Stand.*, *Non-stand.* and *Substand.* (reflecting standard dialect), *Bot.* and *Mus.* for 'Botany' and 'Music' (reflecting field of discourse), *coll.* for 'colloquial' (reflecting tenor of discourse), and so on. The suggestion here is that definitions and citations for dictionary entries can be linked to a more delicate statement of their dialectal and diatypic provenance as a guide to their appropriate usage. Such work by lexicographers might release the *American Heritage Dictionary*, for example, from feeling the necessity of falling back on a panel of 'experts', from all walks of life, as arbiters of what is, or is not, acceptable. There is often only a narrow line between what can be seen as the informed intuition of the native speaker and his accumulated prejudices. Neither are so good as a guide to appropriate usage as are situationally sensitive observation and description.

In statements of meaning in regard to specific texts

Implicit in the framework for placing and comparing texts which has been put forward in this book is the notion that every text, when seen in its full setting, is individual and distinctive. Every text will also, viewed in this light, have an infinitude of meaning. Semantics must take account of this, and recognize that the purposes for which a text is being examined will determine which areas of the total meaning will be emphasized and exposed. A statement of meaning made with a view to inter-lingual translation would be likely, when compared to one made for the elucidation of native speakers, to select different aspects of relevance, a different ordering of shared relevancies, and different extra-textual features as having a bearing on interpretation. Situationalization is a key not only to the fuller understanding of individual texts, but also to the development of semantics.

It may be said in general that the native speaker's linguistic competence is a competence in a host of varying circumstances. Any model of linguistic competence which takes a de-situationalized view of language activity is that much impoverished. Competence-dominated linguistics faces the danger of sidling into psychology; performance-dominated linguistics of drifting into sociology. The one focuses on language as human behaviour, the other as social behaviour; but linguistics is perhaps most itself and preserves its integrity most successfully when it focuses on language as human, social behaviour, when it has a balanced concern both with modelling linguistic competence and with what actually happens in situations, patterns discoverable in the records of language events. A constant recourse to the records of such events, records of both phonic and graphic substance, and of possibly relevant extra-textual features, is perhaps the key to balance. The language event, being both a manifestation of competence and an instance of performance, must remain our point of departure and return.

It has not been possible in a book of this size to give more than the briefest illustrations of how language varies in relation to its social context. What illustration we have given has been largely drawn from English, partly because this is a book written in English for an English-using readership, and partly because English is one of the most important, widespread, and socially complex languages in the world. The general categories we have suggested for dealing with dialectal variety may not all be relevant to all languages. It is possible to conceive of a linguistic community where geographical provenance plays no part in language variation; it is also possible to conceive of a language existing in a community with no social distinctions; certainly questions of standard and non-standard are not necessarily universally applicable, and the notion of code has so far only been examined in relation to English. But all languages seem to show variation along the dimensions of time (temporal dialect) and individuality (idiolect); and the diatypic varieties (field, tenor and mode) and the concept of register, related as they are to the major functions of language (ideational, inter-personal and textual), are here asserted to be applicable to and revealing in the description of all languages. We hope our readers have been encouraged to look around them, to listen, read, and find their own exemplifications, and that they have been helped to organize their observation and understanding of what are those constant features of user and use which are related to language variation.

Appendix

The recording of text used here was made in a student-operated café/pub on the campus of a bilingual (English/French) university college. The majority of the surrounding community is anglophone but bilingual students, faculty and staff do not hesitate to use French to francophones or to each other within the college community. Some of the following text will therefore be in French and there will be several examples of code-switching in the sense of switching from one language to the other.

We are interested, of course, in the relationship of field, mode and tenors to the text itself. The field is that of the purchasing of food, drink, etc., in a pub. The vocabulary reflects this: there are references to particular types of food, brand names of cigarettes, etc. The functional tenor, what the user is doing with language, is instrumental in nature, that is to say that the customer is using language to obtain a desired object. Different personal tenors operate with each customer/staff relationship. This is usually shown in the text through the use of given names for address. There are as well some interesting examples of language-switching which reflect personal tenor. Among the different statuses that are relevant in this particular environment is that of bilingual or monolingual. Because of the location of the college most monolinguals are anglophone. Bilingual francophones will therefore vary their choice of language according to their perception of the addressee's competence in French. The informal egalitarian relationship existing between customer and employee is also shown, through tenor, in the casual nature of the interaction. The employee can openly tease the client in a good-natured way. The atmosphere is very relaxed.

Phonetic notation was not used for this text since this did not seem necessary for our purposes. Intonation is, however, marked by the use of arrows, ⌐ indicating rising intonation, ⌐ indicating falling intonation. This was, of course, necessary because intonation is frequently the sole indicator of grammatical function as in some question forms:

C: un thé⌐
S: encore⌐ ... merci⌐ yes Dave⌐
D: coffee⌐
S: two⌐
D: yeah⌐
S: thirty⌐ thank you⌐ ... well it really doesn't matter because yes⌐
C: two coffees please⌐

Here we see two quite typical transactions. A request is placed in French by an individual who recognizes that the request will be understood; in other words the employee's status is defined as bilingual. The response 'encore⌐' is an exophoric reference to a previous transaction. The switch to English signals a new transaction just as 'merci' signals the termination of the previous one. The use of the customer's given name establishes the relative informality of the customer/ employee relationship. The question 'two⌐' is again exophoric reference. There are two people present, one request only has been made and clarification is required. Again 'thank you' terminates the transaction. There is an immediate pick-up of a continuing conversation between the two employees working together. There is no need to qualify, for example by saying 'In answer to your previous question ...', nor is there any need to go back as it were and start again. A conversation is interrupted (as they frequently are) by the arrival of a customer, here signalled by 'yes'.

D: are you going to transcribe the whole thing⌐
S: yeah it won't take long⌐
D: uggh⌐ ... hi⌐
S: thirty please well I'm not it's not going to be complete⌐ you'll know whether it's falling or rising

C: do you have coke↗

S: rising or falling intonation but that's all

D can continue the conversation in spite of the interruption and like S can talk as well to the customer, e.g. greeting. Again there is the exophoric reference typical of spoken conversation: 'the whole thing', 'it's'; there are the false starts of conversation: 'I'm not it's not'; and the fillers: 'well'.

D: yeah↘ . . . I wonder how come he doesn't have cans of pop↗

S: well we had↗ a coke machine but they took it out↘

D: when was that↗ . . . oww↗ yeah↘

S: the beginning of the year↘ it was sitting there↘ well it never worked which was why it got removed↘

The 'yeah' terminates this conversation. The ensuing question begins another one related to the question of the previous customer who, incidentally, did receive a response. In this instance the reply was non-verbal, a slow shake of the head. The exophoric reference here is interesting: 'he' refers to the pub manager, this is understood; 'they', on the other hand, does not refer to anyone in the experience of either of the participants. It is the 'they' general, the 'they' of other, the 'they' of authority, the 'they' of official 'cokedom'. This difference is implicit and yet perfectly well understood. The 'there' is more situation-bound. This exophoric reference refers to the place where the machine was located within the vision of the two participants.

C: excuse me↗ I hate to do this but I'm bringing it back 'cause it's stale↘

S: ow well I'll make you another one↘

C: ok↘ thanks a lot↘ I I kinda feel bad doing that but

D: I guess so eh↗ (laughter) well it's your own fault↗

C: I do↘

S: is that more to your liking↗

C: yeah ok well I feel rotten bringing it back↘

D: well no↗

overlap
{
S: well if you're not satisfied you should why should why should you eat something you've paid for
C: I know
S: if you
C: I know
S: don't want it 'cause it's not . . . fresh
}

In this sequence the exophoric 'it' refers to a type of bread known as a bagel. We have what is often considered to be a clear indexical marker of Canadian English, the filler 'eh' plus rising intonation. Indications of spoken conversation include interruption of speech, e.g. D: 'well no', and overlap, e.g. the final series SCSCS, also hesitations and more false starts.

S: coffee↗
C: not for me I don't drink coffee↘ I'll have ahh apple juice
F: no I get mine for nothing↘ there you go↘

This sequence illustrates the extent to which gesture and facial expression coincide and often replace verbalization. The fact that F (another staff member) has served himself a coffee is enough to provoke the question 'coffee↗' of the customer who has entered with F. Here the word means 'and do you want coffee too?' Disapproving facial expression forces F to explain why he is not paying for his coffee, i.e. 'no I get mine for nothing'. 'there you go' concludes the transaction.

S: oui Marie↗
M: uhh deux gros duMaurier et un Export A s'il vous plait↘
S: trois↗ non deux↘
M: deux gros duMaurier puis un grand Export A↘
S: bien tu peux avoir au moins un↗ . . . uhh
D: No cream in here eh↗ . . . do you want any more↗
C: yeah↘
D: Susan going for cream↗ Fred↗ is Susan going for cream↗ yeah↗ . . . what can I do for you↗
M: ow uh large duMaurier king size↘

S: you want another one↗
M: yes but there's no more↘ I think Susan has gone to look for it↘
D: ow . . . she's gone for it↘
F: she's gone to get cream↗
D: yeah↘
F: ow↘ ok↘
D: can I help you↗
C: je veux avoir . . . two ham and cheese on a kaiser↘
S: c'est le c'est le dernier paquet↘
M: ok donne-moi un petit↘
D: do you want me to hand you the thing Gilles↗
M: et puis donne-moi uh . . .
D: ow they've taken it↘
M: potato salad potato salad ↘
S: ok↘ no there's no basket↘ Stuart broke it last night↘
D: oww
S: and Fred's already taken some out↘
D: ow↘ . . . ow↘ . . . ow↗ ow↗ ow↘ do you want mustard or mayonnaise↗
C: mustard↘
D: on both of them↗
C: uh yes↘
S: merci beaucoup↘ next please↘

This final series illustrates just how much language can occur during a single transaction between a customer and an employee. The 'oui Marie' being a single transaction, the 'merci beaucoup' concludes it. It is interesting to note how infrequent is the use of personal address in face-to-face contact. S can refer to Marie directly by name since they are well acquainted but when D addresses herself to M she uses the more formal 'can I help you↗'. Use of French is a recognition of M's status. Given names are used to refer to someone absent, e.g. 'Susan going for cream↗', 'I think Susan has gone to look for it↘' and also to gain attention, e.g. 'Fred↗', 'do you want to hand you the thing Gilles↗'.

There is an interesting case of code-switching in this section. A francophone, deeply in conversation in French, is interrupted by the initiating phrase 'can I help you'. The customer begins in French, recognizes the anglophone status of the addressee and switches to English. Another type of switch occurs, too. M wishes to order something she habitually refers to in English, i.e. potato salad. She hesitates somewhat and then orders in English after having spoken in French and then repeats the lexical items as if to reassure herself about them.

There are some linguistic games being played here. D is frequently teased about her manner of expression and at one point catches herself indulging in one of her most frequent characteristic uses, e.g. 'ow'. Hearing herself repeat the filler several times in succession she purposely repeats them again rhythmically like a chant and altering the intonation.

In this example of language-in-action we see that language is an important feature of the situation but ancillary to it. There is more exophoric than endophoric reference; most of the social activity can occur without accompanying linguistic interaction; initiating and concluding phrases although ritualistic are very important. And these are true of much of the language we really use in many social contexts.

Some suggestions for further reading

A simplified and well-exemplified introduction to varieties distinction is *The Language People Really Use* by James Benson and William Greaves (Agincourt, Ontario, Book Society of Canada, 1973). In this respect Randolph Quirk's *The Use of English* (London, Longman, 1962) has stood the test of time well and makes excellent reading.

Investigating English Style by David Crystal and Derek Davy (London, Longman, 1969), *Cohesion in English* by M. A. K. Halliday and Ruqaiya Hasan (London, Longman, 1976), and Waldemar Gutwinski's *Cohesion in Literary Texts* (The Hague, Mouton, 1976) are, in their different ways, all of prime importance as regards the study of texts in their linguistic and social contexts.

The relationships between varieties of language in different contexts of culture and geographical provenances, and problems of standard language are discussed in *The English Language in West Africa*, edited by John Spencer (London, Longman, 1971), and in G. W. Turner's *The English Language in Australia and New Zealand* (London, Longman, 1966).

English in Advertising: A Linguistic Study of Advertising in Great Britain by Geoffrey N. Leech (London, Longman, 1966) is a revealing examination of a set of complex contemporary registers, and Norman Page's *Speech in the English Novel* (London, Longman, 1976) raises questions as to how the creative writer makes use of the relationships between varieties of language and literary and social contexts.

J. C. Catford's *A Linguistic Theory of Translation* (London, Oxford University Press, 1965) demonstrates the necessity for an articulate framework of variety distinction in the process of translation.

Martin Joos's classic essay *The Five Clocks* (The Hague,

Mouton, 1962) and Dell H. Hymes's *Foundations in Sociolinguistics: An Ethnographic Approach* (Philadelphia, University of Pennsylvania Press, 1974) and 'Models of the interaction of language and social setting' (*Journal of Social Issues*, 23, 1967) are pertinent contributions from American scholarship.

The place of language-variety theory and description in the wider context of socio-linguistic and general linguistic theory has been best dealt with by M. A. K. Halliday (see Bibliography) particularly in *Explorations in the Functions of Language* (London, Arnold, 1973) and *Learning How to Mean: Explorations in the Development of Language* (London, Arnold, 1975).

Bibliography

The following is not intended to be a comprehensive bibliography of works relating to language variation and social contexts, but as details of the references cited in the chapters of this book.

ABERCROMBIE, D. (1955), 'English Accents', *The Speech Teacher*, 4, pp. 10–18.

ABERCROMBIE, D. (1963a), 'Conversation and Spoken Prose', *English Language Teaching*, 18, pp. 10–16; reprinted in D. Abercrombie, *Studies in Phonetics and Linguistics*, London, Oxford University Press, 1964.

ABERCROMBIE, D. (1963b), 'Pseudo-procedures in Linguistics', *Zeitschrift für Phonetik*, Sprachwissenschaft und Kommunikationsforschung, vol. XVI; reprinted in D. Abercrombie, *Studies in Phonetics and Linguistics*, London, Oxford University Press, 1964.

ABERCROMBIE, D. (1967), *Elements of General Phonetics*, University of Edinburgh Press.

ALEXANDER, P. (ed.) (1951), *William Shakespeare: The Complete Works*, London and Glasgow, Collins.

BAILEY, C. J., and SHUY, R. W. (eds) (1973), *New Ways of Analyzing Variation in English*, Washington DC, Georgetown University Press.

BASSO, K. H. (1970), '"To give up on words": Silence in Western Apache Culture', in P. P. Giglioli (ed.), *Language and Social Context*, Harmondsworth, Penguin Books, pp. 67–86.

BENSON, J., and GREAVES, W. (1973), *The Language People Really Use*, Agincourt, Ontario, Book Society of Canada.

BEREITER, C., and ENGELMANN, S. (1966), *Teaching Disadvantaged Children in the Pre-School*, Englewood Cliffs, New Jersey, Prentice-Hall.

BERNSTEIN, B. (1970), 'Social Class, Language ad Socialization', in P. P. Giglioli (ed.), *Language and Social Context*, Harmondsworth, Penguin Books, pp. 157–78.

BERNSTEIN, B. (1971), *Class, Codes and Control, Vol. 1: Theoretical Studies Towards a Sociology of Language*, London, Routledge & Kegan Paul (Primary Socialization, Language and Education Series).

BERNSTEIN, B. (ed.) (1973), *Class, Codes and Control, Vol. 2: Applied Studies Towards a Sociology of Language*, London, Routledge & Kegan Paul (Primary Socialization, Language and Education Series).

BERNSTEIN, B. (1974), 'Introduction' to *Class, Codes and Control, Vol. 3: Towards a Theory of Educational Transmissions*, London, Routledge & Kegan Paul (Primary Socialization, Language and Education Series).

BICKERTON, D. (1973), 'Quantitative versus Dynamic Paradigms: The Case of Montreal, Que.', in Bailey and Shuy (eds) (1973), pp. 23–43.

BLOCH, B. (1953), 'Linguistic Structure and Linguistic Analysis', in A. A. Hill (ed.), *Report on the Fourth Annual Round Table Meeting on Linguistics and Language Teaching*, Washington DC, Georgetown University Press, pp. 40–4.

BRITTON, J. N. (1970), *Language and Learning*, London, Allen Lane (The Penguin Press).

BROWN, R., and GILMAN, A. (1960), 'The Pronouns of Power and Solidarity', in T. A. Sebeok (ed.), *Style in Language*, Cambridge, Mass., MIT Press, pp. 253–76.

BÜHLER, K. (1934), *Sprachtheorie: die Darstellungsfunktion der Sprache*, Jena, Fischer.

CATFORD, J. C. (1965), *A Linguistic Theory of Translation*, London, Oxford University Press.

DANĚS, F. (ed.) (in press), *Papers in Functional Sentence Perspective*, The Hague, Mouton.

EARLY ENGLISH TEXT SOCIETY (1891), *The Old English Version of Bede's Ecclesiastical History of the English People*, original series, no. 96, trans. Thomas Miller, London, Oxford University Press.

EDWARDS, L. F. and GAUGHRAM, C. R. L. (1971), *Concise Anatomy*, New York, McGraw-Hill.

ELIOT, T. S. (1959), *On Poetry and Poets*, London, Faber.

ENKVIST, N. E. (1964), 'On Defining Style', in Enkvist, Spencer and Gregory (1964).

ENKVIST, N. E., SPENCER, J., and GREGORY, M. J. (1964), *Linguistics and Style*, London, Oxford University Press.

FIRTH, J. R. (1935), 'The Technique of Semantics', *Transactions of the Philological Society*, 1935; reprinted in Firth (1957).

FIRTH, J. R. (1937), *The Tongues of Men*, London, Watts & Co.; reprinted in Firth (1964).

FIRTH, J. R. (1950), 'Personality and Language in Society', *The Sociological Review*, 42, pp. 37–52; reprinted in Firth (1957).

FIRTH, J. R. (1957), *Papers in Linguistics*, Oxford University Press.

FIRTH, J. R. (1964), *The Tongues of Men and Speech*, Oxford University Press (reprints of *Speech*, London, Benn, 1930 and *The Tongues of Men*, London, Watts & Co., 1937).

FRIES, C. C. (1952), *The Structure of English*, New York, Harcourt Brace Jovanovich.

GARDINER, A. H. (1932), *The Theory of Speech and Language*, Oxford, Clarendon Press.

GARVIN, P. (1959), 'The Standard Language Problem—Concepts and Methods', *Anthropological Linguistics*, vol. 1, no. 3, pp. 37–41.

GILBERT, S. (ed.) (1957), *Letters of James Joyce*, New York, Viking Press.

GOFFMAN, E. (1963), *Behaviour in Public Places*, New York, Free Press and London, Collier-Macmillan.

GOFFMAN, E. (1971), *Relations in Public*, New York, Basic Books.

GREGORY, M. J. (1965), 'Old Bailey Speech in *A Tale of Two Cities*', *A Review of English Literature*, 6, pp. 42–55.

GREGORY, M. J. (1967), 'Aspects of Varieties Differentiation', *Journal of Linguistics*, 3, pp. 177–98.

GREGORY, M. J. (1969), *What is Good English? A Linguist's View*, Agincourt, Ontario, Book Society of Canada.

GREGORY, M. J. (1972), *English Patterns: Perspectives for a Description of English*, Toronto, York University. Preliminary version, 1966.

GREGORY, M. J. (1974), 'A Theory for Stylistics—Exemplified: Donne's "Holly Sonnet XIV"', *Language and Style*, vol. VII, no. 2, pp. 108–18.

GUMPERZ, J. (1966), 'Linguistic repertoires, grammars, and second language instruction', *Monograph No. 18. Report of the Sixteenth Annual Round Table Meeting on Linguistics and Language Study*, Washington DC, Georgetown University Press, pp. 81–91.

GUTWINSKI, W. (1976), *Cohesion in Literary Texts*, The Hague, Paris, Mouton.

HALLIDAY, M. A. K. (1967), 'Notes on Transitivity and Theme in English', parts I and II, *Journal of Linguistics*, 3.

HALLIDAY, M. A. K. (1969), 'Functional Diversity in Language, As Seen From a Consideration of Modality and Mood in English', *Foundations of Language*, 6.

HALLIDAY, M. A. K. (1973), *Explorations in the Functions of Language*, London, Edward Arnold.

HALLIDAY, M. A. K. (1974), *Language and Social Man*, London, Longman (Schools Council Programme in Linguistics and English Teaching, Papers, Series 11, 3).

HALLIDAY, M. A. K. (1975a), *Learning How to Mean: Explorations in the Development of Language*, London, Edward Arnold.

HALLIDAY, M. A. K. (1975b), 'Language as Social Semiotic: Towards a General Sociolinguistic Theory', in A. Makkai and V. B. Makkai (eds), *The First Lacus Forum*, Columbia, South Carolina, Hornbeam Press.

HALLIDAY, M. A. K. (forthcoming), 'Text as Semantic Choice in Social Contexts', to appear in T. A. Van Dijk and J. B. Petofi (eds), *Grammars and Descriptions*, Berlin and New York, De Gruyter.

HALLIDAY, M. A. K., and HASAN, R. (1976), *Cohesion in English*, London, Longman.

HALLIDAY, M. A. K., MCINTOSH, A., and STREVENS, P. (1964), *The Linguistic Sciences and Language Teaching*, London, Longman.

HANDSCOMBE, R. J. (1970), 'George Herbert's "The Collar": A Study in Frustration', *Language and Style*, vol. III, pp. 29–37.

HASAN, R. (1973), 'Code, Register and Social Dialect', in Bernstein (ed.) (1973).

HAUGEN, E. (1966), 'Dialect, Language and Nation', *American Anthropologist*, 68, 4 August, pp. 922–35.

HAVIANEK, B. (1964), 'The Functional Differentiation of the Standard Language', in P. Garvin (ed.), *A Prague School Reader on Esthetics, Literary Structure and Style*, Washington DC, Georgetown University Press.

HEMINGWAY, E. (1970), *Islands in the Stream*, New York, Scribners.

HUXLEY, A. (1937), 'The Language of War', *Collected Essays*, New York, Harper & Row.

HYMES, D. H. (1967), 'Models of the Inter-action of Language and Social Setting', *Journal of Social Issues*, 23.

HYMES, D. H. (1974), *Foundations in Sociolinguistics: An Ethnographic Approach*, Philadelphia, University of Pennsylvania Press.

JESPERSEN, O. (1909–49), *A Modern English Grammar on Historical Principles*, vols I–VII, London, Allen & Unwin.

JESPERSEN, O. (1933), *Essentials of English Grammar*, London, Allen & Unwin.

JOOS, M. (1962), *The Five Clocks*, The Hague, Mouton.

LABOV, W. (1966), *The Social Stratification of English in New York City*, Washington DC, Center for Applied Linguistics.

LABOV, W. (1970), *The Logic of Non-Standard English*, Georgetown 20th Annual Round Table Conference on Linguistics, Monograph 22, pp. 1–43, Atlantis, Georgetown University Press.

LABOV, W. (1972a), *Language in the Inner City: Studies in the Black Vernacular*, Conduct and Communications No. 3, Philadelphia.

LABOV, W. (1972b), *Sociolinguistic Patterns*, Philadelphia, University of Pennsylvania Press.

LABOV, W. (1973), 'The Linguistic Consequences of Being a "Lame" ', *Language in Society*, 2, pp. 81–119.

LABOV, W., COHEN, P., and ROBINS, C. (1965), *Preliminary Study of English Used by Negro and Puerto Rican Speakers in New York City*, Co-operative Research Project 3091, New York, Office of Education.

LABOV, W., COHEN, P., ROBINS, C., and LEWIS, J. (1968), *A Study of the Non-Standard English of Negro and Puerto Rican Speakers in New York City*, Final Report, Co-operative Research Project 3288, vols 1 and 2, New York, Office of Education.

LAMB, S. M. (1966), *Outline of Stratificational Grammar*, Washington DC, Georgetown University Press.

LAMBERT, W. (1967), 'A Social Psychology of Bilingualism', *Journal of Social Issues*, 23, pp. 91–109.

LEVIN, S. R. (1962), 'Suprasegmentals and the Performance of Poetry', *Quarterly Journal of Speech*, XLVIII, pp. 366–72.

LYONS, J. (1963), *Structural Semantics*, Oxford, Blackwell.

MALINOWSKI, B. (1923), 'The Problem of Meaning in Primitive Languages', supplement I in G. K. Ogden and I. A. Richards, *The Meaning of Meaning*, London, Routledge & Kegan Paul.

MALINOWSKI, B. (1935), *Coral Gardens and their Magic*, vol. II, London, Allen & Unwin.

MARTINET, A. (1965), 'Peut-on dire d'une langue qu'elle est belle?', *Revue d'esthétique*, nouvelle série 3–4, pp. 227–39.

MENCKEN, H. L. (1936), *The American Language: An Inquiry into the Development of English in the United States*, New York, Knopf.

MITCHELL, T. F. (1957), 'The Language of Buying and Selling in Cyrenaica: A Situational Statement', *Hesperis*, 44, pp. 31–71.

MORRIS, D. (1967), *The Naked Ape*, London, Cape.

NEMSER, W. (1974), 'Approximate Systems of Foreign Language Learners', in J. C. Richards, *Error Analysis: Perspectives in Second Language Acquisition*, London, Longman.

ORTON, H. (1962), *Survey of English Dialects: Introduction*, Leeds, E. J. Arnold.

ORWELL, G. (1945), 'Politics and the English Language', in *Shooting an Elephant and other Essays*, New York, Harcourt Brace Jovanovich. Reprinted in J. F. Littell (ed.) (1971), *The Language of Man*, Evanston, Ill., McDougall Littell, to which page reference is given.

PALMER, F. R. (ed.) (1968), *Selected Papers of J. R. Firth, 1952–59*, London, Longman.

PHILIPS, S. U. (1972), 'Participant Structures and Communicative Competence: Warm Springs Children in Community and Classroom', in C. B. Cazden, V. P. John, and D. H. Hymes (eds), *Functions of Language in the Classroom*, New York, Teachers College Press, pp. 370–94.

PIKE, K. L. (1967), *Language in Relation to a Unified Theory of the Structure of Human Behaviour*, The Hague, Mouton.

QUIRK, R. (1955), 'Colloquial English and Communication', in B. Ifor Evans (ed.), *Studies in Communication*, London, Secker & Warburg.

QUIRK, R. (1962), *The Use of English*, London, Longman.

QUIRK, R., GREENBAUM, S., LEECH, G., and SVARTIK, J. (1972), *A Grammar of Contemporary English*, London, Longman.

ROBBINS, B. (1970), *Man's Many Voices: Language in its Cultural Context*, New York, Holt, Rinehart & Winston. See 'Black English', pp. 117–33.

ROSS, A. S. C. (1954), 'Linguistic Class Indicators in Present-Day English', *Neuphilologische Mitteilungen*, Helsinki.

ROSS, A. S. C. (1956), 'U and Non-U: An Essay in Sociological Linguistics', in N. Mitford (ed.), *Noblesse Oblige*, London, Hamish Hamilton.

ROSS, L. (1961), *Portrait of Hemingway*, Harmondsworth, Penguin Books.

SELINKER, L. (1974), 'Interlanguage', *International Review of Applied Linguistics in Language Teaching*, vol. 10, pp. 209–31, Heidelberg.

SMITH, D. M. (1973), 'Creolization and Language Ontogeny. A Preliminary Paradigm for Comparing Language Socialization and Language Acculturation', in Bailey and Shuy (eds) (1973), pp. 287–96.

SOLZHENITSYN, A. (1973), *The Gulag Archipelago*, New York, Harper & Row.

SPENCER, J. (1965), 'A Note on the Steady Monologuy of the Interiors', *A Review of English Literature*, 6, pp. 32–41.

SPENCER, J., and GREGORY, M. J. (1964), 'An Approach to the Study of Style', in Enkvist, Spencer and Gregory (1964).

TODD, L. (1974), *Pidgins and Creoles*, London, Routledge & Kegan Paul.

WARBURG, J. (1961), *The Best Chosen English*, London, Communications Research Centre.

WEGENER, P. (1885), *Untersuchungen über die Grundfragen des Sprachlebens*, Halle.

WHORF, B. L. (1956), *Language, Thought, and Reality: Selected Writings of Benjamin Lee Whorf*, ed. John B. Carroll, Cambridge, Mass., MIT Press.

WOLFRAM, W. (1973), 'Objective and Subjective Parameters of Language Assimilation Among Second Generation Puerto-Ricans in East Harlem', in R. Shuy and R. W. Fasold (eds), *Language Attitudes: Current Trends and Prospects*, Washington DC, Georgetown University Press, pp. 148–73.